CW00684661

DEACON BLUE
JUST WHAT I FEEL

Also by Dave Bowler and Bryan Dray

Genesis: A Biography
U2: A Conspiracy of Hope
The Cure: Faith

DEACON BLUE

JUST WHAT I FEEL

Dave Bowler & Bryan Dray

SIDGWICK & JACKSON

First published 1995 by Sidgwick & Jackson

an imprint of Macmillan General Books
25 Eccleston Place London SW1W 9NF
and Basingstoke

Associated companies throughout the world

ISBN 0 283 06247 9

A CIP catalogue record for this book is available from the British Library

Typeset by CentraCet Limited, Cambridge
Printed and bound in Great Britain by
Mackays of Chatham PLC, Chatham, Kent

To Mom and Dad

For having far more love and
patience than was good for
them and far more than I
deserved

and for Denise

I love that you get cold when
it's 71 degrees and I love that
you are the last person I want
to talk to when I go to sleep
at night.

Always

David

To Trish, Emma and Rebecca for their
love and support. And to Mum, Dad, Gran,
Joyce and Wal without whom this would
have been impossible.
Bryan

ACKNOWLEDGEMENTS

Numerous people have been of the greatest assistance in bringing this book to its final conclusion. Among these are our agents, Tanja Howarth and Charlotte Oldfield, who have been remarkably patient in dealing with our assortment of queries and embryonic nervous breakdowns.

At Sidgwick & Jackson, Helen Gummer and Ingrid Connell have both had a considerable input and for their help we are truly grateful.

For encouragement over many years, Mrs Enid Fisher deserves special mention too.

In the course of our research, a number of publications have been of the greatest value, and so we would like to express our gratitude to *Melody Maker*, *New Musical Express*, *Sounds*, *Vox*, *Hot Press*, *Q*, *The Times*, the *Guardian*, *Record Mirror*, *Smash Hits* and Caledonian Newspapers Limited: and to John Waters for permission to reproduce material from *Race of Angels* (Fourth Estate), and Tony Benn for a quote from *The End of an Era* (Hutchinson). We should like to express our particular thanks to the staff of the editorial library at Caledonian Newspapers for their courtesy and speedy assistance.

Denise Dean has again done sterling work in transcribing interviews, uncovering new lines of enquiry, reading the text and making suggestions. Without her assistance the book would never have been completed, but this is no guarantee of a pay rise.

Our families have of course been pillars of strength and it is only with their considerable forbearance that we were able to continue. They have our eternal thanks.

This book was written on an IBM PS/1 with Microsoft Works software. The time has come to upgrade things a little. Any chance?

INTRODUCTION

Deacon Blue, in the course of a relatively short life of just eight years and four 'proper' studio albums, managed to divide musical opinion in a way few other groups of their stature have done. If the critics were initially supportive, the spite they unleashed with unrestrained glee as the group's career unfolded was far more vituperative than the standard backlash all artists have to suffer. It suggested either a hidden agenda of aggression towards the mortgage-sensible, CD-buying rock generation of which Deacon Blue were perceived to be standard-bearers or alternatively that the bile was justified against a band which had given up artistic integrity in return for a healthy bank account.

At the same time, the further Deacon Blue have fallen from critical grace the more successful they have become commercially, nonchalantly replacing the material girl herself at the head of the album charts in 1989 when she was at the peak of her powers. Their success continued into the 1990s unabated; if anything, a Deacon Blue release was as eagerly awaited as those of any of those traditional rock heavyweights whose appearance sets cash tills ringing the length and breadth of the land. Deacon Blue were acquiring a seemingly ever-increasing audience that was always keen to catch up on the group's development.

It's hard to reconcile the two viewpoints – journalistic

jaundice regularly leads to the inescapable conclusion that selling lorryloads of albums inevitably means compromised, sold-out, bland corporatism. Given the evidence of the past decade, it's an idea that's eminently understandable, even forgivable, as the likes of Dire Straits and Pink Floyd have captured the world's markets with shiny, sanitized production values that give the impression of rock 'n' roll without any of the grit, the sweat, the fervour that gives the whole experience real meaning. Ersatz rockers peddling virtual reality rock have been the staple of the new marketing values which have permeated the music world since the advent of the compact disc. CDs may have provided us all with improved sound quality – though some might disagree – along with greater convenience but their most lasting impact has been to rescue a dying record industry. When the compact disc player became the essential addition to every home, the older generation of ex-rock fans who had long ceased to be regular consumers of contemporary music needed something to play on their new prize possession and the marketing men were able to sell them their record collection all over again, but this time on shiny, happy discs. With this older audience now being enticed into the music shops they hadn't frequented since the days when Richard Branson only sold records, the companies saw a gap in the market for a more mannered, very adult, sophisticated kind of pop music. It is into this category that the press have generally deposited the hapless Deacon Blue. The apparent absence of any radical posturing or enigmatic utterances on the band's part has only exacerbated the problem, since the critics have had no obvious pegs on which to hang favourable comments.

Few would disagree with the fact that Deacon Blue have occasionally embraced the virtues of 'production' a little too warmly, squeezing the humanity from their muse and music, sometimes veering uncomfortably close to plasticized soul, providing their detractors with an arsenal of ammunition with which to pound them. The conventional wisdom then suggests that in consequence, their audience must be a dispassionate one which sees their records as some kind of lifestyle choice, mood music for washing dishes or polishing a coffee table.

It should be simple to dismiss Deacon Blue as a mere yuppie accessory that lasted beyond their appointed decade. Yet their audience is fiercely partisan, their concerts sell out quickly and their records leap straight into the charts. These are all hallmarks of a group that means something to its audience, whose members are in direct communication with their peers, a direct contradiction of everything which we are led to believe represents their style of music.

Deacon Blue are an anomaly, a group out of time in some respects. In many record collections, they rub shoulders with the likes of Van Morrison, Bruce Springsteen and U2, none of whom have been short of a few critical plaudits. In others, they nestle alongside Whitney Houston and Michael Bolton. There are people with the former collection who would have their records fumigated if they even suspected that one of Whitney's CDs had spent a moment in the same room, while many of Mr Bolton's supporters wouldn't recognize the myriad attributes of a U2 album if you tattooed a list on their forearms. How then do Deacon Blue bridge this credibility gap?

To cover this ground, it's necessary to define the terms on which Deacon Blue are to be dealt with. For the purposes of this book, Ricky Ross, lead singer and major songwriter, is taken to be almost synonymous with Deacon Blue. This is not to impugn the considerable contribution that the other members of the troupe have made to the band's musical or commercial development. It is simply a reflection of his overwhelming input and leadership and an acceptance of the way the wider audience has come to treat the group. Few bands in the modern world succeed without having a focal point and that is generally the lead singer. Some encourage the attention, while others try to deflect it.

Had the promotional machinery not been largely centred around Ross – vocal foil and eventual partner Lorraine McIntosh later taking a share of the spotlight – it's hard to see just how

Deacon Blue would have reached the heights they did. Personality is a crucial facet in promoting a band to the world; for instance, of their contemporaries, only Wet Wet Wet have gone on to real success, based on the central character of Marti Pellow while other touted and talented performers such as Danny Wilson or Hue and Cry have fallen by the wayside, slipping into the charisma-void which denies them TV and radio exposure, the lifeblood of any self-respecting marketing strategy. To the world at large, Ricky Ross is Deacon Blue and Deacon Blue is Ricky Ross.

That advertising ethic has been part of their problem, of course. The publicity machine through which Deacon Blue passed did its job in terms of ensuring a healthy financial return on the considerable investment that was channelled into them. Marketing might can be a double-edged sword, though, and so it proved with Deacon Blue. Campaign after campaign pushed the group further forward to a wider and wider audience, simultaneously leaving critical commentators cold with the calculating commerciality of it all. CBS, both before and after their takeover by Sony, attacked the market place as though they were selling fish fingers rather than music. Their newly-serious artist George Michael was sufficiently affronted by their behaviour to try to escape their clutches via a long-drawn-out, ultimately futile legal battle. The appropriate marketing departments can of course claim with some justification, indeed pride, that Deacon Blue did scale the peaks of success with a couple of No 1 albums and three others which reached the top four, while it was marketing skills that rescued their debut album from obscurity and possibly saved their career.

The presentation of Deacon Blue as an 'album band' was somewhat out of step with the late eighties when even those artists who had previously largely ignored the singles format began to see it as a useful method of attracting a new audience. It was in these terms that Deacon Blue's singles output was regarded – mere tasters, three-minute adverts for the current album, an album which would then be subjected to the hard sell. For that reason, they enjoyed relatively little success in the singles chart for such a successful band with only the 'Four Bacharach & David Songs EP' achieving a top five position. If this was an understandable strategy from the record company standpoint, from the wider view it led to a thorough misunderstanding of the band and what they were trying to represent.

As 'serious' artists they were derided by a press who, understandably perhaps, reserved that tag for the likes of REM, Neil Young, Lou Reed or U2. Deacon Blue did not really fit into that rather stern mould for their songs were unselfconsciously grounded in the pop field, something for which they rightly made no apologies. Had Deacon Blue's singles been given a greater profile and treated as more than advertising fluff, they may have won fairer treatment for themselves and earned another and rather different audience, for the singles were generally excellent examples of pop songwriting and performance with little trace of pretension or pomposity while the B-sides often illustrated a group with a sense of humour, a wider musical frame of reference than was generally credited, and a willingness to experiment with different approaches to songs. Closer examination of the B-sides would have revealed cover versions of songs by Julian Cope and Hüsker Dü, a measure which might have endeared the band to a knowledgeable musical audience. Sadly, this was an opportunity that was all too rarely taken, a marketing mistake which was to have serious repercussions for the future of the group.

When the time came for Deacon Blue to attempt to broaden their musical palette and tackle new subjects, new sounds and new styles with the release of their fourth studio record, *Whatever You Say, Say Nothing*, the markers that were put down by the accompanying singles were disregarded simply because Deacon Blue had already been firmly placed within one musical category by the style of marketing and publicity that had accompanied earlier releases. Singles by Deacon Blue were not supposed to be treated as significant since past experience had already indicated that the record company wanted people to part with album-sized bundles of cash. Certainly, the album format gave the complete picture of what Deacon Blue were striving for in totality, but the refusal to see singles as anything other than trailers to win a little radio play was deeply flawed. Just imagine if U2's singles had been promoted in such a lackadaisical way; if 'The Fly' had escaped rather than been released, the musical world would not have been alerted to the seismic shift that *Achtung Baby* represented. Many people who regained an interest in U2 by virtue of that radical departure would have been denied the opportunity to reassess them if the approach had been, 'Ho-hum, here's another U2 single.' The striking departure which *Whatever You Say, Say Nothing* represented for Deacon Blue, one heralded by the extremely unlikely but highly imaginative selection of new dance gurus Paul Oakenfold and Steve Osborne as producers, was ignored by a wider audience who might have found much to admire within the fresh and highly contemporary music that filled that album. The previous non-believers were never properly presented with an opportunity to re-evaluate the group.

As it was, few outside the Deacon Blue fold were willing to listen, a legacy of the lax policy on singles promotion in the past, allied to the merciless pushing that the albums had had; a complete turn-off for those who dislike the hard sell. People missed out on the surprising vitality of the myriad remixes that accompanied the singles, which would have provided a way into the albums. Worse yet, their B-sides were packaged onto albums not once but twice by the record company, allegedly in response to demand. The consequence was that from the outside, it appeared that Deacon Blue fans were being cynically milked for every penny they had, simultaneously suggesting, however wrongly, that the group felt that every piece of work they completed was a major statement that justified album status. This provided ideal fodder for the band's detractors.

In fairness, not all the blame for the group's later problems can be laid at the door of the record company. Indeed, the band's release of their most notable single, 'Real Gone Kid', was almost tantamount to signing their own death warrant. Although it only reached No 8 in the charts, the song, with its insistent chorus, was probably the most played single of the year with a hookline that remained lodged in your mind whether it was welcome there or not. Its bold, brassy production was indicative of the whole album from which it sprang, *When the World Knows Your Name*, an album which reaped the whirlwind of success on the back of that nagging advert, which seemed to bear out everything that had been written about Deacon Blue's premeditated, totally calculating assault on success. This was a band that would sell its soul for an extra sale, or so the story went.

Written seemingly from insecurity, *When the World Knows Your Name* was a misguided attempt on Ross's part to earn security of tenure at the record company with a succession of hit singles which would further pump up the sales of the parent album, thereby ensuring that CBS would continue to foot the bill for further recordings. Once Ross had presented CBS with a golden marketing opportunity and the image of a band at the forefront of some spurious 'new rock' movement, hindsight suggests that he inadvertently closed the door on commercial and artistic progress travelling harmoniously in tandem, and gave the public an image of Deacon Blue that was to be set in tablets of stone, for better or worse.

It's possible to suggest that Deacon Blue were commercialized to death, set inside a corporate strait-jacket that they could not escape. As a far more unorthodox and idiosyncratic songwriter and musician than public perception would suggest, it was perhaps inevitable that Ricky Ross would rail against these confines and seek to slip his ties by calling a halt to the band. As such, Deacon Blue provide a wider warning for the music industry as a whole. By inaccurately presenting an artist for short-term gain, the longer-term potential can be lost. Given the enormous cost of launching a new artist on a largely indifferent population, it is surely foolhardy in the extreme to do anything to reduce their artistic life. Pigeonholing may provide a useful reference point, a launch pad from which sympathetic support can be gained, but it eventually creates a prison which is anathema to the creative artist.

At their heart, like all but the unabashed teen sensations, Deacon Blue were a wilful group out to make their own music on their own terms in their own way. At its head, Ross was an eclectic and talented tunesmith who had far more to offer than he was given credit for. Imagemongers came between the music and the audience and this ultimately spelt the band's demise. That they refused to go beyond their inevitable Greatest Hits collection, itself an obvious marketing ploy to regain ground lost by the ineffective promotion of *Whatever You Say, Say Nothing*, was a shame. Their legacy is a surprising variety of musical styles which clearly meant a great deal to a great many people and which said much about the decade in which they worked.

CHAPTER ONE

When you look at Deacon Blue and their music from a present day perspective, it's very difficult to see anything other than a band that was always destined for major-league success, one that couldn't fail to top charts and sell out concerts the length and breadth of the land. All the ingredients appear to be in place: a conventionally attractive frontman with a strong, bluesy voice and a penchant for writing unashamedly romantic hooks; his vocal foil, a vivacious young woman who, for added spice, was later to become the frontman's wife; a solid band behind the two, seasoned players of taste and ability able to colour in the sound sympathetically to bring out the very best from the material provided while they also offered an added depth with their backing vocals in live performance. How could a group that was to dominate both the album charts and the radio airwaves in 1989 and was able to rack up a platinum-selling hits collection five years later have ever struggled to get people to listen to them?

Within the music business it has become almost axiomatic that before any budding artist or group can finally place their hands on the much sought-after recording deal, they must first accumulate a sheaf of rejection letters from every other player in the industry. The Beatles were overlooked, most famously by Decca, U2 were rejected by many UK companies, Springsteen had his share of 'thanks but no thanks' slips and so the list goes on. If Deacon Blue didn't go on to have the eventual worldwide impact that those artists did, they nevertheless had to endure similar withering indifference from a recording industry that seemed blind to the blatantly commercial nature of the band's talents.

Those decisions look particularly foolish in the light of the vast quantities of 'units shifted', to appropriate that especially obnoxious piece of music industry phraseology. Ricky Ross was to recall later that Phonogram had told him that they wouldn't even sign the group for 50p! It wasn't until 1986 that CBS, in the shape of director of A & R, Muff Winwood, finally produced the contract and a long-term strategy for the group's future. As a former musician himself, having played in the Spencer Davis Group in the sixties, and having a highly talented brother in Steve Winwood, Muff was able to recognize all the hallmarks of a top-class songwriter.

CBS had tracked the group for a while, watching them play a number of live showcases, seeing them exercise their potential on the live stage, ensuring that it would not be a rash decision to sign this much-ignored band. When they did agree to take the band onto their roster, Ross admitted that they were the only company that had made any offer.

The inking of legal papers was the culmination of years of struggle for all concerned, but most notably for Ricky Ross, lead singer and prime songwriter within the group and an artist who had been treading the boards from his middle-teens a decade earlier. As the group's central motivational force, it fell to Ross to keep things going in the face of corporate indifference. His was the job of maintaining internal morale while honing the songs that would eventually lead to the group being signed. Fortunately, personal discipline and a belief in his own ability were virtues that Ross possessed in spades, in no small part a result of a highly distinctive and rather unusual background, an upbringing that was to stand him in good stead for life in the volatile pop industry.

Ricky Ross was born in Dundee on 22 December 1957, and his childhood was a little unconventional compared with that of his contemporaries. The differences centred around the religious foundation on which his family life was built: the teachings of the Christian (or Open) Brethren Church. Though the adherents to the faith were geographically disparate, living all over Dundee, they formed a tightly-knit community that made light of physical distance and forged strong bonds between each other.

Ross later explained some of the religion's roots to Mat Snow of *Q*. 'The Christian Brethren came out of nineteenth-century philanthropy, children's homes and all that. To understand it, you have to imagine Southern Baptist sensibilities in America: no smoking, no drinking, no football on Sundays. That's obviously skimming the surface; it's not just a series of don'ts.' Even so, it's clear that living within that form of religion instilled moral values into the young Ross, values of honesty and dignity which were later to come tumbling across the pages of his lyric books. The concept of community was central to his later philosophy too, illuminating many of the songs on records such as *Raintown* and *Fellow Hoodlums*.

It's an important element in the Ross story, so the ethos of this faith bears some explanation. As Ross stated, it grew up in the last century and has its roots in the Plymouth Brethren, a Protestant denomination which initially sprang up in Dublin in 1825 as a reaction to a highly sectarian age. It tried to formulate a basis for Christian unity, it abhorred the closed communion practised within denominations. It believed that factions should be forsaken rather than merged and that people could meet simply as Christians whatever their differences. The message was taken to Great Britain by John Nelson Darby, a godson of Admiral Nelson, and a preacher in the Church of Ireland. Nelson's zeal tended to alienate others in the faith and there was a division in 1848 which led to the formation of the Christian Brethren, who opted for a more relaxed style than the dogmatic leadership imposed by Nelson.

The beliefs of the Brethren were most notably characterized

by the strongly puritanical attitude of which Ross was speaking. Their distrust of popular entertainment was a particular feature. Time and the advent of the mass media have contrived to chip away at this resolve, though Ross did recall, 'With my parents, it was always a struggle; they would never say, "Here's a few quid, go and buy a keyboard." To them, pop was the worst option; the important thing was safety in your job.' Even so, the Brethren faith is not as extreme as this, or its failure to become more widespread, might suggest.

The guiding principle of the Plymouth Brethren, a principle with which the Christian Brethren have kept faith, is that the Scriptures are the tenets by which people should live, organized religions with their doctrinal formulations having come between people and the true word of God. They hold that it is not necessary to have appointed clergy following formalized orders of service in order to take communion. For that reason, their places of worship do not always carry the name 'church', for they recognize that a church is not a building but the people who meet together; thus these meetings often take place in Bible Chapels or Gospel Halls, a preferred term.

The Christian Brethren in particular have developed a fierce determination to evangelize, while serving society is central to their beliefs. As Ross has explained, they had important roles to play in the establishment of orphanages and charitable institutions in the last century, and the concept of service to the community remains strong within the faith. In their departure from the stricter dogma of the Plymouth Brethren, the Christian Brethren have been able to espouse the virtues of community and co-operation towards a mutually desired end.

As an evangelical faith the Brethren have regularly engaged in foreign missionary work as well as immersing themselves in social works at home. This concept of communal enterprise is of course a central feature of Ross' work as a writer and as a member of a group – it's interesting to note that while the Brethren do not have any ordained ministry, the autonomous local congregations encourage anyone who is clearly capable of an educational or evangelical role to develop those talents to the full. It is common within the Brethren that those who do develop in this way will regularly travel to other congregations throughout the country, providing an exchange of theological ideas which ensures the vitality and evolution of the faith. Thus connections are made between communities worldwide. Is this not what a rock band, especially one motivated by global issues as strongly as it is by personal financial ones, strives to achieve? The teachings of the Christian Brethren are not exclusive, for members are willing to join not only with other congregations, but with churches of other denominations when they feel the need arises – again an ideal which Ross was to follow in his attempts to embrace a wholly disparate audience with Deacon Blue's music.

Growing up within such a comparatively strict regime, many would have been tempted to strike out against the conventions, yet Ross was able to embrace the faith for much of his youth. 'As a teenager growing up with it you have two choices: you go along with it or you rebel. I stayed with it a long while, I think because I believe very strongly, I'm an interminable believer!' Behind this hint of self-mockery, however, there's a real grain of truth as his musical career has gone on to prove. If there are few vestiges of overtly religious evangelicalism in Deacon Blue's songs, there is often a strong spiritual undercurrent that distinguishes them from the standard popular music fare of the time – other ephemeral popsters of the late-eighties and early nineties had little truck with such values, preferring to embody the Thatcherite legacy in their naked pursuit of money and success.

That said, it's a thin line between aiming for success to utilize the opportunities it can provide to help other people, and cultivating it for purely selfish gain. The Christian Brethren church had characteristics that might have been surprising for such a philanthropic organization. 'There's a very typical class group who tend to end up in the Brethren: the cliché used to be that it was self-employed men and their wives and that would be largely true. My father is one such person – home-owning, car-owning, insurance policies, lower-middle-class.'

The Brethren's puritanism was coupled with the prevalent Protestant work ethic that is a feature of the dominant Presbyterian Church in Scotland. With their humanitarian instincts, the Brethren realized that they could best help the poorer elements of society from a position of financial strength and security. This can be distorted to represent an endorsement of the 'trickle-down' theory of economics embraced by a capitalist system in that a philanthropic richer class will take care of the disadvantaged underbelly of society but in truth the idea is closer to a microcosmic form of socialism in its devotion to community and collective responsibility.

Having attended one of Dundee's better schools and having had a materially secure childhood within a lower-middle-class household, Ross has always been wary of falling into the trap of playing the 'working class hero', a position which would be false and contrived. It is nevertheless a tag which was foisted upon him, generally without success, in the aftermath of records such as *Raintown* and *Fellow Hoodlums*, with their concentration, superficially at least, on working-class culture. Certainly he has flirted with the cloying sentimentalization of the working class predicament at times – an affliction that soured the work of people like Paul Weller and the Clash for instance – but he is sufficiently grounded in the realities of that kind of life to be able to steer clear of the temptation in most cases.

Robert Sandall of *The Times* was later to describe Ross as 'socialistically stern and Sting-like' and it's an understandable reaction to his sometimes overpowering sincerity, but these are the hallmarks of his upbringing. The most obvious manifestation of this was the way in which he initially suppressed his musical ambitions in order to look for a more settled and responsible career as a teacher. He attended teacher training college in his native Dundee following which he helped set up a youth club for local kids with nowhere else to go which was financed by a local church. Quite clearly this was a logical extension of the teachings of the Christian Brethren but by this stage, Ross was thinking in more political than religious terms. Political activity on both a local and world stage was something which inspired Ross, yet any political commitment was tempered by the Brethren's fundamental rejection of doctrinal affiliations.

From a political standpoint, his interests were on an individual level, as his songs were to reveal later with striking eloquence. When Central America was making the news with ominous regularity in the mid-eighties, by which time Ross was involved in the music scene, he organized a benefit in aid of Nicaragua; or rather, to raise funds for a friend who was going out to offer concrete, hands-on assistance to the people of that troubled nation. Ross has generally stayed on that path, being far more concerned with the work of the individual than faceless groups. It has sometimes made him seem naive or drawn the criticism that he is out of touch with wider events, but it has nevertheless served his songwriting well, keeping that human element as a constant that people everywhere can identify with. Ross has never wanted anything but to address the 'universal themes' in his songwriting.

Ross went in to teacher training college at the tail end of the 1970s, just prior to the Conservatives coming to power. Their election and the havoc that Thatcherite dogma began to wreak on towns and cities, especially in Scotland and the north of England, naturally had an impact on his outlook. To begin with, it was soon made abundantly clear that there was no longer any such thing as a secure job for life, which must have eaten away at his determination to see his training through and enter a working environment. More importantly, he was to see at first hand the devastating results of the culture of greed and the free market economy which closed down older industries without ever seeking to put anything in their place.

A fierce patriot, Ross has always been devoted to Scottish interests, particularly since as a nation state Scotland has received such a raw deal at the hands of Westminster politics – with the notable exception of the 1974–9 Labour government. This provided Scotland's greatest opportunity in recent history for some form of devolution and control over its own destiny, yet in the last days of that Labour administration, a referendum in Scotland failed to gain the requisite number of votes needed to set up the Scottish Assembly, in the wake of some highly distorted anti-Assembly propaganda. Consequently, for a short period, Scottish nationalism was in retreat, the wind taken from its sails.

However, as Conservative policies seemed to strive to destroy industrial communities in Scotland, it quickly became clear that there was a vital role for nationalism to play after all, one of energetic protest at the running down of an entire nation by a government that had no mandate within the country; the Tories being a minority party north of the border. There was much to be fought for within Scotland itself, as jobs were destroyed with great glee by those for whom tax cutting for the wealthy outweighed the obligation to support the needy through the welfare state. This played a critical role in further politicizing the young Ross.

If he felt that teaching might have been an important, invigorating or interesting way of fighting back, this was a feeling that was gradually being eroded by his interest in music and, most notably, in songwriting. This is not to say that Ross came to music as an evangelist, hoping to change the planet with his songs, but rather that as the world as he had known and come to terms with had changed, his response to it had necessarily to change too.

Most important of all, he found himself freed of the shackles of responsibility and was keen to follow his own drives. He was to say later that, 'If you wanna be in a band, you wanna be in a band,' and it's clear that it was a long-held dream of his, to operate within the music industry to take his ideas onto a broader stage. Having obtained qualifications, the security that his parents had wanted for him and which he clearly wanted for himself, he felt that he had the opportunity to cast his net wider.

This at last was the rebellion against his background which might have been expected earlier in his life.

Ross had already noted that he received little encouragement from his family with regard to the prospect of a musical career and pop's less than spotless reputation for maintaining a high moral tone must have been a factor in their distrust of the medium. That he should have gone to college rather than joined a band at eighteen is very much a legacy of the Brethren's philosophy, centred firmly around communal rather than personal aspirations.

In this regard, there are striking parallels between Ross and Bono of U2. Bono has regularly confirmed that he was actively discouraged from dreaming, from having ambitions above the norm, by his Catholic father. He has come to see that this was simply a protective cloak thrown around him by a man who knew that he was more likely to be forced into conforming to society than permitted to exist beyond its normal confines. It was a philosophy also reinforced by Bono's own experience of the Plymouth Brethren, the stricter strain of the faith. Bono's close friend Derek Rowan, later to re-emerge as Guggi of the Virgin Prunes, was a member of that faith and his family were particularly strict adherents to its code. Bono would regularly spend time with them, anxious to hear more about their beliefs in order to see if they might apply to his own life.

The combination of his father's caution and this new teaching had a number of effects on Bono, but due to his eclectic background – a Protestant mother, Catholic father and a place at Ireland's first multi-denominational school – he was able to mix and match elements of each philosophy to arrive at his own decisions. To him, Christian belief suggested that he should make full use of his gifts and therefore he reacted violently to the idea that he should conform to the nine-to-five and know his place in society. For Ross, it took longer to break free of these restrictions, these ideas that had been drummed in to him, for he was brought up to have no material ambition, ambition being regarded almost as sinful since it suggested avarice.

As is inevitable in the cause and effect cycle, once Ross did choose to rebel against his background, though rebel is possibly too strong a word for one who had already carefully prepared a safety net for himself, he attacked this new option with extreme fervour. Having suppressed his ambitions for so long, and having exerted considerable personal discipline in repressing those desires, once he unleashed them he became a chronic over-achiever, always striving to make up for lost time to prove wrong the pessimists who doubted his talents. It was this that was misinterpreted in the light of *When the World Knows Your Name* as a soulless crusade in search of financial success, a yuppie-style disregard for anything other than commercial interests.

It's easy to infer that Bono's need to succeed has always been at least partly a gesture to a society that tried to pigeonhole him. One of Ross' heroes, Bruce Springsteen, came from similarly cautious stock. For Springsteen, however, rock 'n' roll was viewed as a more legitimate form of escape from drudgery, a means of avoiding a blue-collar life. Springsteen's lyrical concentration on life as a highway is not coincidental, since in American mythology the car has always represented freedom, a freedom that he sought as a restless spirit. Ross was, by his early twenties, of similarly independent mind. While he could understand and appreciate the tight-knit community of Dundee's Brethren, and while he would draw on this heritage as a musician, it was too restrictive. As a creative artist, Ross needed space to breathe and to give free rein to his talents. In this sense he was following the Brethren's evangelical path in fully developing his abilities and taking them out into a wider world.

The Christian Brethren's way of life does influence his songs as he attests. 'I used to get really hung up about my background when I was young. I used to think it had no romance. Compared to the other kids at school, it always seemed so dull . . . when you're young and you read other people's experiences of life – James Joyce living in Dublin, George Orwell living in Burma – you begin to think, "How could your experiences compare?" Then you realize that they're just taking one experience and magnifying it and you begin to value your family and background and realize that they are unique. You have to realize these strong points . . . I reached a turning point when I realized that my background was actually quite rich and quite unusual. I realized then that everybody's background could be as interesting as they wanted it to be.'

Continuing in the same vein, Ross remembers that, 'I decided to think of my own in more colourful terms and that gave me a great inheritance in words, phrases and experiences that I still draw on when I'm writing songs. One of the things that I like about Bruce Springsteen is the way that he brings his own background to life on songs like "Independence Day" and "The Ties That Bind". Once you grow up enough to accept and come to terms with it, your background can be a great thing.'

While parallels are being drawn between Ross, Springsteen and Bono, all are passionate performers which has been both their most endearing characteristic and the source of critical flak. Bono has seen the music of U2 as a healing force in a country divided by religion. His ambition has always been to unite, to reach out to people and invite them into the group's music. Ross has been a similarly outgoing character. Bono hit the nadir of his critical popularity with *Rattle and Hum* when it was felt that he was too overbearing, too desperate to be all things to all people. In the wake of that backlash against 'sincere rock' in 1988–9, Deacon Blue released their most thoroughly produced record, their most blatant stab at commercialized stadium music. They were duly obliterated in the critical storm as Ross' proselytizing from the stage was no longer *de rigueur* behaviour for a rock star.

Yet Ross had not changed, times had simply moved on with the studied cool of Madchester's Stone Roses and Happy Mondays then being the order of the day. This was sad in many ways since that warm-hearted approach has largely been dispensed with in the intervening years and musical cliques built on exclusion have been constructed. The Christian Brethren were, ironically, a faction that split from the original Plymouth

Brethren faith. The other faction is sometimes referred to as the Exclusive Brethren. An artist like Ricky Ross would have no truck with exclusivity since it would negate everything that music represented for him.

Writing songs has always been important to Ricky Ross, an interest that dates right back to the late sixties. In the light of that, it's interesting to see just why he accepted the conventional path that his roots determined. In going to teacher training college, was Ross fulfilling his own ambitions or was he simply trying to appease a family that wanted him to accumulate the necessary qualifications to gain a safe job for his future? Many factors are at play; he was naturally keen to please his parents and prove to them that he was capable of taking a responsible place in society.

His choice of teaching as a future career clearly betrays the lasting impression that life within the Brethren community had on him – if he was not taking an evangelical religious message out to the wider world, he was at least striving to help educate children and thus equip them for a successful future. This is a prime example of his community-based ideals, helping enrich the local environment with ideas and assisting youngsters in standing on their own feet for their own future benefit, an evangelical mission of its own in such turbulent times.

In 1981 at the age of twenty-four, and 'very naïve, amazingly immature', he finally decided to leave his home town of Dundee for Glasgow with his wife Zara to work with a new band called Woza, while supporting himself by teaching children with behavioural difficulties in the Maryhill district of the city. It was a long time since he had first become attracted to music, awoken to its incredible potential by his older sister's record collection as he informed Mat Snow. 'About the first record that came into the house after Beatles singles was *Electric Ladyland*. It blew my mind! I had no other reference points. Then I remember when *Abbey Road* came out. I still love that record. From listening to that is where my expectations of making a record come from; the ideal album should flow and have a cohesion.'

His departure to Glasgow and a position in a new band was not Ross' first attempt at treading the boards. *Melody Maker*'s Tom Morton recalled his first sighting of Ross on stage in Dundee in 1977, performing his Springsteenisms before a live audience. 'I remember buying *Born to Run*, unwrapping it. I remember the smell of that album . . .' was a typical Ross line, one which speaks volumes about his attitude to music and to his heroes. Although it took several years more before he was in a position to play on stage with a group that was looking to make a mark within the industry, the fire had always been alive in Ross' heart, the desire to follow Bruce or Van Morrison onto the stage and tread in their footsteps. Ross was finally on his way.

CHAPTER TWO

There are few things in life more soul destroying than having to take work to earn sufficient money to subsidize your hobby, a hobby which you would like to turn into a full-time career. If you feel that the hobby is not progressing as it should and that you could be making greater strides if only you were in complete control, then this becomes an increasingly depressing experience.

Having relocated to Glasgow for a fresh start, Ricky Ross inevitably found that he had to continue working as a teacher in order to pay for his musical obsession, at least until things began to take off. While he found teaching English a rewarding job in parts, he found it increasingly frustrating. He was to reflect later that, '[my] last proper job . . . was teaching in a secondary school in Maryhill in Glasgow. I certainly didn't hate it, but I disliked the way it took up such an inordinate amount of my time. There was always a slight feeling of wanting to get away from it.' By now Ross was thinking of himself as a song-writer first, musician second and a teacher third. These priorities held an important distinction for Ross since it amply illustrated just what he felt to be the vital ingredient in creating timeless music.

When he was growing up, 'My sister was into James Taylor, Carole King, Simon & Garfunkel, and I liked the idea of singer-songwriters; it stuck in my head that they were more important than, say, Tom Jones because they wrote songs. These are my two big influences: the desire to do an *Electric Ladyland* – to rock out – and the desire to hold the song as of paramount importance.' In another age, Ross might well have found himself a spot in Tin Pan Alley churning out popular songs for a host of artists and there's very definitely a part of him that would settle for just that kind of life. For one who grew into such an ebullient, larger-than-life stage performer, Ross has a highly cultivated taste for the shadows of anonymity.

Working as a teacher by day and with Woza at night had its problems but at least it gave Ross the opportunity to play music in front of a live audience and to air some of his own songs. His already forceful character was evolving rapidly and while he took his part in the Woza set up, he quickly began to fret that he was not in control of the group and its activities.

Woza took their name from the anti-apartheid play, *Woza Albert!* Its black South African cast took on myriad roles during the course of the work, including P. W. Botha, then as leader of South Africa, the upholder of the apartheid tradition. The *New Musical Express* once described *Woza Albert!* as 'South Africa's most radical ever slice of drama'. Sadly Woza were not a similarly radical force, playing fairly formularized pop which Ross later described as 'playing what we thought record companies would like'.

To be fair to Woza and its members, who included Ewen Vernal on bass and Brian McGlynn as singer and guitarist with Ross as keyboard player, 1984 and 1985 were not great years to be attempting to make the breakthrough into the pop industry from a Glasgow base. Scotland as a whole had had its turn in the national game of musical chairs a few years earlier when the scene which developed round the Glasgow-based independent record label, Postcard, brought forth Edwyn Collins' Orange Juice and Roddy Frame's Aztec Camera as the new saviours of popular music. As with each new musical scene that bursts into the pages of the music press, it lived its short but useful life and then disappeared. By the mid-eighties, the focus of musical attention had, in pop terms, moved on to the glitz and glamour of Duran Duran, Culture Club, Wham! and Spandau Ballet, while the rock axis had shifted towards Manchester with New Order and the Smiths. Glasgow was relegated to its more customary position, so far as the industry was concerned, of musical outpost with only the raucous advent of the Jesus and Mary Chain creating any sizeable waves.

The Postcard set-up had in some respects given a false picture of Scottish music. Both Frame and Collins were undeniably gifted songwriters but both had a tendency to head towards coy, rather fey, jangly arrangements which did not capture the more traditional grittiness of the nation's music. Frame's whimsical subtlety was much favoured through the early part of the decade, though he lost much of his impetus when he took a three-year break between records, by which time pop had moved on from the 'coy wimpdom of the jangling juveniles' as Adrian Thrills termed it. By 1985 Scotland was represented on the international stage by the leaden thud of Big Country's allegedly rousing swirl of guitars, and Simple Minds, who had finally made the leap into the American charts with 'Don't You Forget About Me'. On the smaller scale, the smooth jazz sound of Hipsway – 'a designer white-boy funk spawned by the Glaswegian club scene' as *NME* dismissed it – was the most likely music to make any impression south of the border, not a piece of news to stir the hearts of A & R men in their cosy London offices.

Woza were working around the 'new pop' blueprint, taking a few leaves from the Roddy Frame book and by 1984 local observers felt that they might be on the verge of greater things, but the band dissolved over a period of months owing to the legendary 'musical differences'. They were back together again by the following year and a *Melody Maker* live review suggested that 'this time, nearly everything is right', going on to inform the readership that Woza were 'fresh, new and bursting with potential'.

Although the group was seemingly on the brink of a breakthrough, Ricky Ross was far from happy with his lot in the band. In 1984, as Woza were temporarily disintegrating, he had put together a tape of songs called *So Long Ago* with a view to gaining a publishing deal.* The tape illustrates that as early as 1983/4 Ross was already a formidable songwriter, his intricate yet powerful melodies overcoming the obvious limitations of a tiny recording budget. The songs are generally in the reflective, downbeat style that was to characterize 'Raintown' a few years later, often based around piano rather than guitar. In a song such as 'Some People Last Winter' with its refrain detailing broken-down people, Ross was clearly exploring the themes of *Raintown*, that song an obvious precursor of his lyrical thrust on that début album. Ross clearly had a firm grasp on the rudiments of songwriting, occasionally recalling the likes of Billy Joel or Phil Collins on the brassy 'I Love You Like a Son', although the low-key nature of much of the material might have caused A & R men to pause for thought since in its finest moments it owed more to the understated tenor of John Martyn's work. Certainly, Ross was Woza's leading songwriter, Tom Morton remarking, 'The occasional dodgy lyric cannot detract from the quality of material such as "Stranger at the Party" or the mystical "Echoes of Another World" although Ricky Ross' "Big Shoes" is the set's obvious high point.'

Songwriting was Ross' main pursuit at this stage but as keyboardist in what was, to all intents and purposes, someone else's band, he felt that his creativity was being stifled while Woza itself would not be able to make the necessary transition to a professional recording group while it simply shadowed whatever movement was popular at the time. Bluntly, Ross felt that his writing ability was far greater than that of anyone else within the band and that he should be fronting the group,

* The songs were: Something About Ireland / A Week in Politics / Checkout Girls / Don't Look Back / Little India / Surprised By Joy / Some People Last Winter / Vision On / I Love You Like A Son / The Germans Are Out Today / Chairman Mao's Vacation.

notwithstanding a review which suggested that Brian McGlynn was 'a great singer (Elvis via Van Morrison) and a charismatic performer.'

Van Morrison was of course a major influence on Ross both as a writer and as a singer and their Celtic heritage was a shared bond. Another common characteristic was their determination to do things properly, by which each man means to do things their way insofar as is possible. From similar lineage is John Martyn, possibly the finest songwriter that Scotland has produced, though he and Ross diverge in Martyn's desire to use the guitar more than his voice, understandable in such a gifted, if under-rated, player. There were to be very clear echoes of Martyn's work as Ross progressed, particularly in terms of the lyrical concerns and the blue-collar perspective. Unlike both Morrison and Martyn, however, Ross has drawn little influence from folk traditions. Woza never dabbled in that genre of music and Deacon Blue never showed any real inclination towards it either.

Ricky Ross was fairly clear later as to why that should be the case and equally dismissive of any criticism that he was failing to address his cultural roots by neglecting the folk tradition. 'I really love the folk tradition of handing down songs from one performer to the next and from one generation to the next. I'd never claim that we were a folk band because it is obvious that we aren't. But I'd like to be able to write songs as good as some of the great folk songs like "Deportees" by Woody Guthrie. There's a hard realism about these songs that is missing from most rock music.

'But we didn't grow up listening to that kind of [Scottish folk] music. Scotland isn't like Ireland. If you're from Ireland and you go to pubs anywhere you can't avoid traditional music. But Scotland is a different highlands and lowlands thing and in Glasgow we're an urban culture. Friends of mine who play in a folk group have to go out and research it. The only exposure I ever had to it was TV programmes on a Friday night. [At one point] I thought about doing a Burns song and it was such a struggle because I realized it couldn't be authentic. The music that I feel most comfortable with is pop music.'

Essentially, Ross' problem with regard to his national cultural heritage is that of anyone who has grown up in the post-Elvis world, a world that has been colonized by America. When Ross was first taking in music in the mid-sixties, he would have had access to a national radio station that, prior to the advent of Radio 1, mixed and matched the Beatles and Elvis with Sinatra and Crosby. The pop charts of the day were equally schizophrenic. It's hard to believe from this distance that the first Beatles single after 1963 not to reach No 1, the 1967 seminal coupling of 'Strawberry Fields Forever' and 'Penny Lane', was kept off the top by Englebert Humperdinck. Meanwhile, what would now be regarded as easy listening in the form of stars such as Perry Como, Petula Clark, Tom Jones and a host of others was regularly charting and doing very well thank you among the Beat stars and their successors in what has solidified into the rock format.

In the 1960s, commercial concerns were powerful formative factors in radio programming, and popular music was pumped out to the masses in a much broader format than that pejorative term now implies. One of Ross' most fêted contemporaries is the admittedly sublime Paddy MacAloon of Prefab Sprout who draws on a similar school of songwriting to Ross; indeed if anything, MacAloon's tastes are rooted even further in the past than Ross'. Cleverly, MacAloon has appropriated stylistic tricks from the likes of Sinatra's arranger Nelson Riddle and yet he has never been castigated for not producing traditional Tyneside airs.

This rather unfair treatment is not a matter that surprises Ross, who is quick to jump at any inference of anti-Scottish bias in the press. Talking with *Melody Maker*, he complained about a headline accompanying a Deacon Blue review. 'It was "Light Macs", 'cos there was a picture of me wearing one. Isn't that the most racist comment you've ever heard coming from a supposedly liberal journal? It was a classic. Southerners are couched in this kind of liberalism and then when it comes to Scotland, we're all jocks together.'

The prejudice against Scottish musicians which Ross perceived – which many would say is a music industry prejudice that extends to anywhere beyond London – convinced him that he would have to work much harder and be much better than the competition in order to make any impact on the wider world outside Glasgow, a dawning realization which led to his increasing frustration at his position within Woza.

As Woza were just going through the motions, in Ross' view anyway, he must have reflected on his motivations for wanting to make a career out of songwriting rather than simply accepting the relative security of life as a school teacher. The chief force that propelled him into the very different world was his belief in music, particularly in good rock music, as a form of both entertainment and also as something more. Ross was drawn towards creating a music that would touch a nerve in people and allow a shared experience to illuminate whatever personal joys or sorrows they were living through.

In that way, it all sounds hopelessly highfaluting and pretentious but to those people who passionately care about their music, it's a simple statement of the truth, a given that guides their lives. Ross nailed his colours to the mast early on, saying, 'I've seen people who work at Charly lovingly take out old records, dust them down and present them as if they were dressing their kids for a Barmitzvah. That's what pop should be like but you can't stand there and rationalize that 'cos clearly it's naked stupidity.'

Thousands of boys in Scotland grow up wanting to score the winning goal in the Cup Final at Hampden Park or the winning try at Murrayfield in the last minute of a Calcutta Cup match. Few give a second thought to a lad who aspires to be Paul McStay or Ally McCoist or, when Ross was growing up, a boy who wanted to be Denis Law. Big football fan though he is, Ross didn't want that. He wanted to grow up to be Van Morrison, Bruce Springsteen, Jimi Hendrix, Mick Jagger, Bacharach *and* David, Lennon *and* McCartney all at the same time. Perhaps Ross' most famous quote in the whole of his career to date, made to *Melody Maker* back in 1986 before Deacon Blue even had a record contract, was 'I wouldn't trust anyone without a decent record collection.' It's that kind of belief, that passion mixed with a twist of arrogance that pushed Ross to the centre stage.

Woza's seemingly inevitable demise was hastened by a couple of formative experiences for Ross as a musician, both involving other groups. Firstly, Woza supported Friends Again, a Glaswegian quintet under the leadership of singer Chris Thompson and guitarist James Grant who eventually went on to front Love and Money. Reappraising their career later, *Q* considered them 'the missing link' between the Postcard sound and the designer funk of Hipsway and Wet Wet Wet with their 'perfect pop' and 'literate and layered, stately arrangements and creamy harmonies'. Ross recalls that they 'were doing exactly what I wanted to do, playing Van Morrison-y songs, slightly country, slightly American, when everyone else was concerned with being post-punk and having an attitude.'

This band and their approach struck a chord with Ross and lodged themselves firmly in his memory banks. The final push that nudged him out of Woza was provided by the remarkable Mike Scott and the Waterboys. 'One of Woza's final gigs,' remembers Ross, 'was supporting the Waterboys on their first gig in Britain in this wee bar in Wishaw. Here was someone who was playing with the same energy, the same passion as Bob Dylan; it was like, punk's over after people had been trying to live in that image for years.'

Yet while Ricky Ross took the advent of Mike Scott as closing the book on a musical movement that had largely passed him by through its lack of what he would term songs, many, many observers took to Scott and his group because they felt that he was returning to that punk period with his ferocious energy while couching the music in more traditional terms – punks with tunes in essence. The Waterboys hold an interesting place in the annals of British music over the last decade, managing to experiment with various stylistic fusions without ever really losing their critical cachet. It's fair comment to suggest that Scott has carefully presented his image as a musical maverick to a wider world while still ensuring that he made sufficient records with a commercial edge to keep the wolf from the door.

Similarly, the fact that Scott had worked with Chrysalis, one of the smaller record companies, has helped protect him from accusations of selling out. In sharp contrast to Ross, whose work on *Raintown* and *Fellow Hoodlums* in particular was not wholly divorced from Scott's own tastes, Scott has been able to maintain his standing critically and commercially through manipulating the presentation of his music more thoughtfully than Ross who has, it must be said, himself been manipulated by CBS and Sony.

When the hype is stripped away and you listen to the Ross canon and that of Mike Scott, it's clear that although they have their musical differences, they are kindred spirits at heart, drawing inspiration from much the same well. Ross' first exposure to the Waterboys was his road to Damascus. It was 'the turning point . . . the key moment when I understood why I had to do it. I was unhappy 'cos I was playing keyboards and the band wasn't going anywhere. The Waterboys were soundchecking and they had their great big rig and I thought, "Who is this bunch o'hippies?" I just remember Mike Scott plugging in and saying, "Right, 'All The Things She Gave Me'" and there was this mighty, mighty noise, an incredible sound and I just went, "Oh yes! Yes, yes, yes!" It really was everything.'

Once Ross had seen the Waterboys, he knew that he had to leave Woza and start afresh, showcasing his own material, having learned a central lesson about music and about himself. Having made his way onto the music scene as a means of entertainment and an escape from everyday drudgery, Ross now had to come to terms with the fact that he wanted to write songs for his own satisfaction and that simply being a member of a group was not an acceptable substitute. Ross had been drawn towards the music industry because the music was in his blood. He had to make his way in life by chasing the sounds that meant everything to him. It was his only viable means of expression and honest freedom of expression was now his goal.

CHAPTER THREE

Once Ricky Ross had made up his mind that he needed as much as wanted a career in the field of songwriting, it meant embracing some harsh realities. In order to find the time necessary to create and then hone a body of new songs, it meant a degree of isolation from family and friends which created inevitable tensions. However, having eventually got eleven songs ready and demoed, he quite quickly secured the interest of ATV Songs.

Looking back to the days of the Brill Building's massive songwriting success with songwriters such as Neil Sedaka turning up for work every day through the 1950s and into the early 1960s to write hit after hit for the likes of Sinatra, Ross would have been perfectly happy, might even have been better suited, to the back-room role, writing and producing songs for others to perform. The post-Beatles rock world, however, insists that performers write and writers perform and so, while ATV Songs were excited by his potential as a songwriter, they insisted that Ross put a group together and play live shows to drum up record company interest.

Playing live is a time-consuming business in itself, but starting from the basics, having to put an entire group together from scratch turns the situation into one of nightmarish proportions. Something within Ross' life had to give and it was his job. Leaving the teaching profession was something of a wrench since Ross enjoyed imparting knowledge to youngsters but at the same time he couldn't say goodbye to the administrative routines quickly enough. He joked that he had quit teaching as a reaction to the long-running teachers strike but admitted, 'It was really time. I tried to get my life away from being dilettante for a long time and I just found myself concentrating more and more on music.'

Dilettantism is an attitude which is really anathema to Ross, diametrically opposed to his creed of diving whole-heartedly into whatever enterprise he is involved with. It is this earnestness which at first endeared him to many sections of the press who were tiring of the frivolous nature of mid-eighties pop and its purveyors. But it was this self same characteristic which eventually damned him too, as the perceived wisdom shifted towards not taking music too seriously after all, ironic cynicism becoming the order of the day. In the backlash that was centred around U2 and Sting, the likes of Ross were not allowed to get off lightly either. Rock's true believers came to be an unacceptable embarrassment to those who wanted their music uninvolving and unemotional.

This was not initially a problem, however, as Ross quickly became a performer that many wanted to see, a rocker that they could believe in, though he was adamant that he did not want their trust. 'The worst thing that anyone ever said about Deacon Blue,' he told *New Musical Express*, 'was that we were a band that you could trust. That sort of thing is just ridiculous! I would never put my trust in a band. I've been let down too many times in the past. Bands should never be trusted.' Such an admission says much about the division between the critical and the commercial audience. While journalists must inevitably deal in the language of hyperbole, favourable or not, those people who have to dig into their own pockets to buy a record or a concert ticket are after other things.

The 'real' audience is fairly loyal, a little more conservative perhaps and very concerned with the important concept of value for money. The public is not constantly in search of 'a group to die for' to quote an oft-bandied phrase from the music press, but rather a group that delivers the goods on a regular basis. If a band or artist can be relied on to perform an entertaining and exciting live show, they'll come back for more and continue to do so until they or the artist becomes jaded, when they'll move on to something else. Critics, however, have to find a group before they gain an audience, create a climate whereby the group can be discovered by a wider public and then, to protect their ground-breaking credentials, move on to something else before the first group has necessarily reached its full potential, going on to snipe at that artist from the island of critical exclusivity which suggests that popular equals rubbish.

Having been a long-time observer of the rock scene, Ross was not a naïve newcomer, about to be consumed by the vagaries of the system. As a mature twenty-eight-year-old, he spent early 1986 trying to set up a group to play his songs so that he could take advantage of ATV Songs' publishing offer and, additionally, secure a recording contract. An early concern was to give this putative band a name. 'I've made up a lot of bullshit about this [name]. The song "Deacon Blues" is very aspirational – the guy wants to play the sax and be James Dean, exactly the same feelings as when you form a band. It wasnae like that at all! I was going down Tottenham Court Road in London and looked over at the Dominion and was very aware that Van the Man used to play there and all of a sudden the name Deacon Blue came into my head – I don't know why. But it had a ring to it and I thought, "I can live with that", even though it was from a Steely Dan song. They're not a big influence.'

Big influence or not, the very name – and it was better than the earlier Ricky Ross and Dr Love – did conjure up a fairly accurate impression of where the group would be heading; into intelligent, mature, adult rock territory with few, if any, concessions to the generally-teenage pop market. Ross admitted as much, while applying political considerations to the eventual shape of Deacon Blue's audience. 'Britain is a changed place,' he said at the end of 1986, just after they had won their recording contract. 'Kids of sixteen and nineteen just aren't buying records any more and that's the fact of the matter. They're buying cheaper, more accessible things . . . the thing that really annoys me the most is we don't get a chance to play to these people. In Glasgow, no one who's not a student or works early in the morning or who looks under twenty-one can get in and see us . . . but I think that all successful bands eventually cross over.'

Crossing over was the least of Ross' worries in early 1986, however. His problems persisted until the tail-end of the year, namely the piecing together of a group that was sympathetic to his music and sufficiently adept at translating it powerfully enough to have an impact on the live circuit. One of the founder members of the group was Dougie Vipond, from Johnstone in Strathclyde, on drums, a classically trained musician who had previously worked with both the Big Dish and the Painted Word. A number of other musicians passed through the group's ranks including Love and Money's John Palmer on guitar, bassist Raymond Docherty from the Big Dish and Carol Moore of Talking Drums, each having assorted lengths of tenure. Ross' unease at the way the group was developing was echoed by Tom Morton in *Melody Maker*, reporting on a gig at Glasgow's Club Eden in March when the band was billed as Ricky Ross and Deacon Blue.

'Now he's got a publishing deal and he's on the verge of that elusive record contract, Ricky is almost entirely right,' wrote Morton. 'His band, however, are entirely wrong. They play competently, cleanly, boringly. In overwhelming contrast to Ricky's heart and soul performance, the arrangements cauterize the songs' passion into Prefab Sprout cleverness . . . the band, it seems, don't understand.'

Having a group of players who were not entirely in sympathy with his muse made life especially difficult for Ross who was, of course, attempting to write new songs while simultaneously trying to grow into this new, semi-enforced persona of frontman.

Not that he seemed to have too much difficulty in adapting to the role. As a long-term student of Springsteen and Costello, he had his approach to live work honed down to a fine art. 'Heroes are on display,' suggested Morton, and certainly the aspirational side of Ross' nature allowed him to dream himself into Bruce's shoes for an hour or so while he was on stage.

This gauche 'let's pretend' kind of approach enabled Ross to gain a reasonable following in Glasgow fairly quickly, while it was also to stand him in good stead nationally later on. Just as five or six years earlier Bono's exuberance and lack of the studied reserve that 'cool' demanded had been a breath of fresh air to audiences on the British mainland, so was Ross in 1986. Here again, there's an element of emulation in Ross' performance on stage, having been highly affected by U2 at Live Aid.

'Funnily enough, I used to hate U2 – so pompous and big – but then I saw the Live Aid video. Now this may sound silly, but it's the only performance I've seen in my life – and I've seen 'em all! – Costello in '78 . . . I mean I've seen some good bands. But U2's performance is the only one I've ever seen that's actually moved me to tears. I don't know why. I didn't feel sad about it but just . . . there was someone, struggling, reaching past all the red tape to get to the punters. Something half sad. Some people would say, "What a prat." But there's something really great about that.'

Ross' identification with Bono in that exceptional Wembley performance makes perfect sense. Both came to rock music from a background of a solid personal faith and were attracted to and intrigued by spiritual ideas. Rather than being repelled by the sometimes excessive nature of the rock beast, both were drawn towards its heart where, in the truly great artists, a real spirituality lurks, even amid those writers who passionately deny the existence of any spiritual force.

There is a magic at the heart of the muse which transcends the sum of a musician's abilities, channelling emotions into a medium which can speak directly to the hearts of listeners without the need for a cumbersome language which in trying to define everything explains nothing. For Ross, like Van Morrison or Bono before him, rock music articulates that spirituality and that faith which each has, which is why it is such a potent force for the good in their lives.

This link goes a little deeper than that, of course. Both Ross and Bono understand the power of ceremony in its religious sense and if they treat its application to music in different ways, Ross sometimes shying away from the authority that it gives him over an audience, they instinctively grasp music's potential for liberating and unifying a crowd, even if just for a brief moment in the course of a concert. Having been steeped in the scriptures and absorbed an all-pervading sense of Christian duty as a consequence of his background, Ross is naturally drawn to unleashing music's capacity as a healing device.

In order to run this to its natural conclusion and to allow it to take its effect, the music has to touch every member of the audience. As the agent of this almost mystical force, Ross found himself struggling to bring an entire audience into the world his music was meant to construct and in consequence, like Bono before him, there were times when he failed and looked faintly ridiculous. But on the nights when he succeeded . . .

Ross quite naturally took an all-embracing philosophy onto the stage with him, welcoming all comers to the concert in the hope of creating such bonds between band and audience and then between the individual members of that audience. Ross described his songs as 'small moments of sadness and instead of making them a bit . . . wanky, making them a bit more sort of communal.'

There is a theme of music as mission that runs through their work too. This is the belief that has led both men along dangerous paths insofar as their credibility is concerned. Such passion can easily be misinterpreted by the unthinking or the mischievous as aimless bluster, pretension or delusions of grandeur. It is the antidote to cynicism, yet cynicism is the very foundation on which the music business, a business which is irrevocably tied to the creation and destruction of spurious fashions, is built. Ross was soon exposed to this in a professional capacity once Deacon Blue were finally making records.

'I did an interview with this guy from Sky Channel and he was just so jaded I felt sorry for him. He'd seen a video of us doing "Dignity" and he was saying, "So, do you think you can sustain that kind of intensity all the way through a gig?" and he clearly thought we were some chest-beating, crashing snare-drum sort of band. I asked him what emotion he meant and he didn't know. He had no control over his language and he'd just used the word emotion to attack us with. And I said, "You sneering bastard. What are you doing here? There's a million emotions in that song and you haven't even listened to the fucking thing."'

Some would look at Ross' anger and find that more appalling than the interviewer's palpable lack of knowledge and preparation. After all, didn't the Stones make the point that it's *only* rock 'n' roll? The problem for Ross is that, just like Bono, he actually believes in rock music, a woefully outdated sentiment among the chattering classes but not among the people that still consume it. To many people rock is still more than just entertainment.

In his illuminating book on Ireland and U2, *Race of Angels*, author John Waters makes the point beautifully:

> What the best modern rock 'n' roll artists show us is that it is possible . . . to preserve the spirit of humanness . . . The contempt of the outside world has led the medium to sell itself short of its own promise. The 'philosophy' of cool has served to divide those elements of life which are aesthetically or politically pleasing from those which are 'merely' everyday, human and necessary . . . There is no point in saying it's *only* rock 'n' roll. Far from being a radical or even cool position, this is merely stupid . . . The irony is that it is people who most *like* rock 'n' roll who say it is 'only rock 'n' roll' and in doing so betray the promise of the music they claim to love by

damning it with low expectations . . . Boogie on down! and don't be annoying me with your angst and ideas.

Musicians like Ross have only ever had the highest expectations of music. Certainly at times Deacon Blue's records have failed to live up to those lofty possibilities but that has never been for the want of trying. Perhaps it is that strain of desperate effort which people see in the straightforward decency of singers like Ross that makes them so popular. Could it be his willingness to fail coupled with his ambition to succeed, not purely in material terms but also on a spiritual level, that so endears him to the many thousands who have taken him and his group to their hearts?

As a singer, Ross is an embodiment of 'everyman', the aspirations and ambitions of an entire audience on display. He has never made any attempt to disguise the fact that he really relishes being able to carve out his existence as a musician and songwriter. It's blatantly obvious that he's on stage having the time of his life and enjoying every minute of the experience, acting out those childhood dreams. A night of playing before a packed Barrowlands Ballroom in Glasgow is like that last-minute winning try at Murrayfield; a sold out show at Hammersmith Odeon equates to scoring a goal at Hampden. Ross has made his dreams flesh and is not afraid of sharing his joy with the people who have put him there. Rock 'n' roll has generally been constructed courtesy of the vicarious thrill, living life at its extremes through the adventures of others. If Ross doesn't chart those extremes, there is nothing vicarious about him and Deacon Blue either. As a member of the audience, you don't watch him enjoying himself, you participate in it.

It's a cliché, it's true, but in seeing Ross make it on to the stage, there is a sense in which he confirms that it is possible for anyone to succeed. That is not to diminish his ability, for his is quite clearly a serious songwriting talent, but in his presentation he is so effusive, so enthusiastic that his presence and ambition are almost contagious. His audience identify with him, the more so in his native Scotland which for the most part has a healthy disregard for the flights of fantastic fashion that cause a feeding frenzy among the London music press. Scottish music is based on older, tried and tested virtues as Ross agrees. 'I don't think you'd ever get people like Stock, Aitken and Waterman coming out of Scotland. It won't happen here – people in Scotland seem to be interested in real bands that can play actual songs, play their instruments and play shows.'

One man clearly capable of playing his instruments was Kilmarnock's James Prime, a widely respected keyboard player who weathered the final days of Altered Images and who had also spent some time working on sessions with John Martyn. He was a relatively early member of the Deacon Blue troupe, signing up in early 1986, soon after his twenty-fifth birthday. His excellent keyboard work helped flesh out Ross' songs and the two were to go on to co-write some of the band's strongest pieces over the years. He understood Ross' vision of Deacon Blue and was pleased to find himself in a band that was in keeping with Glasgow's mood at that time, as Ross conceded.

'If there was a zeitgeist when we got started,' recalled Ross for *Vox*'s Alan Jackson, 'it was that people in Glasgow wanted to hear the song again. They wanted the band to arrive sober and offer up their songs rather than turn up drunk and throw bottles off the stage in the way that I guess the Jesus and Mary Chain had been doing a couple of years before . . . the Blue Nile were the paradigm, I suppose; the Wets when they started. The Big Dish as well; and Love and Money . . . the one strong feeling I always had was for the song, really. Songwriting has a tendency to make itself important in your life. Like smoking or going to the football on Saturday, it becomes one of those things you cannot help.'

Like many others, on joining Deacon Blue Prime was struck by Ross' fierce determination to succeed as well as his songwriting talent. 'When I got involved with this lot,' Prime later remembered, 'the rate of work Ricky and the band were going at was really exciting. I mean, most bands sort of struggle around for their whole careers with something like three songs. This guy had books full of lyrics.' Indeed, it was Ross' prolific nature that was to ultimately lead to such a strong debut album for the group as *Raintown*. Unlike so many debutantes, Deacon Blue had a whole armoury of material to choose from and were therefore able to compile a record that had no obvious weak links.

Even so, the band still had to go through its periods of struggle, playing gigs to a combination of enthusiastic fans and dubious record companies. If Ross' passion for music and performance was the defining characteristic of Deacon Blue, it was sometimes their undoing. It was a problem pinpointed in a live review from June 1986, Tom Morton reporting again, this time from the Royal College of Music and Drama in Glasgow.

'What's stopping them . . . getting a record deal, making money or more to the point being the wonderful band they ought to be? I mean, they've got the songs . . . but the seamless, one-dimensional nature of the set could be blamed on an incipient bent towards fashionability born of desperation and naked ambition . . . Ricky Ross and Deacon Blue could and should be stars. But to achieve that they're going to have to stop wanting success so much it hurts the audience to watch them . . . with less force, the emotion at the root of the Ross muse will come out.'

Morton certainly had a point, but again this leads us back towards Ross' roots. Having given up work in order to further the career of Deacon Blue, it is wholly understandable that he would be keen to get things moving as quickly as possible for his own financial well-being, yet there's more to it than that. The Protestant work ethic, like the Catholic guilt syndrome, is a difficult concept from which to escape.

Furthermore, Ross, though pursuing an alternative career in music, was, from an external perspective at least, unemployed which must have had an effect on him, though his belief in his own ability would have carried him through the darker moments when he must have felt like returning to teaching. Indeed, it was almost certainly as a reaction to these feelings that he worked so feverishly at his songwriting, assembling the formidable canon of work of which Prime spoke. At least by channelling his energies in this way, he was creating concrete proof that he was no idler but someone beavering away at creating a new situation for himself in the future – these songs would be the solid foundations on which his success would be built in the years to come.

The desire to work would not have been Ross' only motivation, though. As was to be demonstrably the case later when writing and recording Deacon Blue's second album, there was more than a suggestion of some deep-seated insecurity gnawing away at this minstrel's heart. It was first visible in these early concerts. Ross needed to see proof from other sources that his work was viable and he did tailor his performances accordingly; they became increasingly desperate as Ross and his cohorts attempted to secure a recording deal and material success.

Ross doesn't appear to be a man who is especially interested in material possessions but is interested in the long-term security and freedom that financial invulnerability offers. The Christian Brethren were, as already noted, self-employed men and their wives from the lower-middle-classes, secure in their professions. Although Ross was trying to escape his roots in one sense, i.e. avoiding the menial grind of the everyday rat-race, it was an accepted tenet that he should make the most of his abilities; success in that sense was not merely the accumulation of material trinkets but a rather more spiritual pursuit, recognizing and developing the gifts given by God. This was a further reason for pushing himself to the limits.

The city of Glasgow and its inhabitants were influencing him too. Some of the sights of the city, sights born of poverty and mass unemployment, forced him to cry out against them. On a live stage before a willing audience, it's a thin line between passionate oratory and empty rhetorical bluster, a line that Ross occasionally crossed in his overwhelming desire to make contact with the crowd. It was something that Ross was trying to come to terms with, saying in March 1986, 'I didn't used to be, but I'm [becoming] a fairly harsh critic of what we do.'

Glasgow did pose other problems for Deacon Blue, though. Ross' passionate and quite obvious self-belief did translate as arrogance at times and his personality was occasionally perceived as too thrusting, too assured. 'It's hard to be honest in any situation,' he confessed, 'but it's particularly difficult in Glasgow. The easiest thing in the Glasgow scene is to be tongue-in-cheek and that annoys me a bit. It seems to be an antidote to failure. If you say you're tongue-in-cheek, you can always pass your mistakes off.' An unflinching honesty in his songwriting was one of the central targets that Ross had set himself and on which he was unwilling to compromise.

There were other drawbacks to living and working in Glasgow. Though Ross might suggest that his adopted city was not fashion-conscious, it did have a feel for what it liked and disliked at any particular period in time. Through much of 1986, Deacon Blue were not entirely the city's favourite flavour, Hipsway and Wet Wet Wet appealing to one faction of musical taste while the Jesus and Mary Chain had already captured another slice of the audience.

Ross understood just what he was fighting against, telling *New Musical Express*, 'There is an incredible pressure on new bands in Glasgow. They are expected to be either a funky white soul band or some mutant offspring of the Velvet Underground. The music that we play is not what the fashionable cliques in Glasgow are into. But that doesn't bother me. You just have to stick to your guns. I think people in Glasgow have started to accept us for what we are . . . once I feel happy with what we're doing, I think other people will as well.'

In order to reach this state of musical nirvana, Ross continued to mix and match the members of the group. It was to be an arduous struggle that persisted throughout 1986 until they finally achieved the necessary alchemy of personalities. The missing ingredients were Graeme Kelling, a twenty-nine year old from Paisley, on guitar, who struck up a friendship with Ross very quickly, based around their shared background, Kelling coming from the Christian Brethren faith too, and Glaswegian, Ewen Vernal, Ross' erstwhile companion in Woza, who took over bass guitar duties. This five-piece began to play more regularly together, developing the areas that they felt were unique about Deacon Blue. Ricky Ross' investment in himself in the form of those long years of struggle around the fringes of the professional music scene was just about ready to pay dividends.

CHAPTER FOUR

The newly formed Deacon Blue quintet of Ross, Vernal, Vipond, Prime and Kelling set about making their name known around the music industry. Ross was undeniably happier with this line-up than any previous grouping he had worked with and the results began to make themselves obvious in a more relaxed approach to live shows, although they lost none of their almost religious fervour on stage. Now, however, they were a group capable of channelling it in the right directions.

Those directions were almost exclusively selected by Ross. It was made clear that having already secured the offer of a publishing contract from ATV Songs, it was to be Ross who called the shots. Although the others made very real contributions to the band sound, and Ross was to collaborate on songs in the future, it was he who set the tone for the group's activities, the way they would progress lyrically and musically. In these early days of the group, this caused no problems since they were all glad to be along for the ride.

Possibly the most significant addition to the band was Lorraine McIntosh, who provided the backing vocals and vocal counterpoint to Ross' lead – which was to become Deacon Blue's trademark sound. She joined the group towards the end of 1986, at the age of twenty-two. McIntosh had already been in bands with Ewen Vernal, their original group Rattling The

Cage becoming Big Sur. Vernal obviously appraised Ross of her potential with the upshot that McIntosh was quickly assimilated into Deacon Blue. For Ross a female voice was an essential element in his musical mix, a predilection dating back to his *So Long Ago* tape.

Having lost both Vernal and then McIntosh, Big Sur were soon to bite the dust, another reason for the degree of antipathy that Glaswegians tended to feel towards Deacon Blue. Ross' ruthless cannibalization of contemporary groups in his adopted home was an integral part of his success, for he had a tenacity of vision and purpose that others might have lacked but his lack of any fellow feeling for other struggling bands did little to endear him to his peers. Glasgow's groups were to become accustomed to losing members to Ross and Deacon Blue and there were hard feelings over the issue. If one can condemn Ross for his merciless attitude, no one was forced to join forces with him. Vipond, Vernal, McIntosh, Kelling and Prime were all won over by Ross' forceful personality and the confidence he had in the future for both himself and his associates. In that sense, the very fact that Ross was so good at recruiting musicians is to his credit and attests to the perspicacity of the musicians in question who recognized a good songwriter when they saw one.

Lorraine clearly saw the potential. 'I was desperate to get into this band,' she told *New Musical Express* in 1988. 'I used to go and see them play live and I'd be singing backing vocals from the crowd. When I was asked to become a member, I just couldn't believe it. Even if I formed my own band I don't think I could love any songs as much as these or get as much out of singing them.' Oddly, given Ross' well reported feminist instincts and his socialist leanings, McIntosh was not given full status in the group immediately. Indeed, even when *Raintown* came out, there was a very definite gulf between her and the five men as far as billing was concerned.

Her voice provided the final missing link between Deacon Blue and the music they were striving so hard to create. Musically, she was also on the same wavelength as the rest of the group as these comments readily illustrate. On Bruce Springsteen's *Tunnel of Love* she noted, 'I was all set to hate it, you know, be all cool and hate the new Springsteen album but there was no way I could hate it . . . it got me straight away and you want it in your veins and inside you and to have experiences to it.'

Her views on Van Morrison were every bit as enthusiastic too. 'Probably my ultimate favourite all-time artist. I remember putting on *Veeden Fleece* over and over again . . . crying my eyes out. "Country Fair" conjures up brilliant memories of childhood and innocence . . . it's absolutely brilliant.' Final proof of her suitability for Deacon Blue comes in an assessment of the Waterboys' *This Is the Sea*. 'It just makes you want to dance about the room. It makes me want to do a gig when I hear that.'

Ross had problems on his plate in trying to convince a record company to sign the band. Financial constraints were very clearly holding the group back as they found it virtually impossible to play concerts beyond Glasgow and almost as difficult to pay the sizeable bill involved in putting on record company showcases in their own city. McIntosh recalls, 'It's a lot of hassle putting on gigs by yourselves when there's no one around to help you, no roadies or anything. No one to even book the gigs for you. And so every time a record company rang up and said, "Yeah, we want to come along and see you," we went, "Oh no, here we go again," and we had to put on another gig. It was a lot of trouble.' Ross admitted to the press that, 'It cost a lot of money as well. It's a very expensive process when the only people who're coming along are your pals and a couple of A & R men, so we had to be careful just how much we did.'

Eventually, fortune began to smile on the group. CBS had paid great attention to Deacon Blue in the light of Ross' relationship with ATV Songs, but their A & R man, Gordon Charlton, had also taken a shine to fellow Glaswegians the Painted Word. It was a chance recommendation by their manager Jill Maxwell that persuaded him to investigate Deacon Blue a little further. Impressed by their demo tape, most notably by the song 'Dignity', Charlton was sufficiently enthused to encourage his boss Muff Winwood to go along to see them in Glasgow. As Lorraine McIntosh remembers, 'We did lots of gigs for the record companies and sent out loads of demo tapes. A few companies came to see us and talk to us but [CBS] were the only ones who wanted to sign us!'

With their immediate future secured by late 1986, Deacon Blue were able to go beyond the confines of Glasgow, playing their first shows in London at the Marquee to rapturous reviews. *Melody Maker*'s Mat Smith commented on 'a nervous energy' in the group that suited 'songs fraught with melancholy and mystique, pride and prejudice, but while Ricky Ross harbours Mike Scott's] inescapable lust for life, he's occasionally prone to [Lloyd Cole's] oft dreadful wordsmithery . . . the emotion that hides behind the cloud of literacy is as vivid as life itself and sung with a howling conviction . . . the best thing to come out of Scotland since Scott and company and will probably be just as durable, sharing as they do a similar sense of ethnic Americana in songs like "Dignity" and "Raintown".'

Ross returned to his home town of Dundee just prior to Christmas 1986 as a kind of celebration of his success. Playing the Dance Factory 'Deacon Blue come on, looking ordinary as expected and then play a bloodthirsty, blockbusting set . . . Ross has made something out of melody, fire and groove that resembles a Springsteen-fuelled Little Feat with razor cuts and soul emotion . . . the band are simply excellent. The vocal cross-over between Ross and a magnificent tiny girl singer are striking enough and the straightforward unadorned excitement they produce is a wonder to behold' according to *New Musical Express*'s Bob Flynn.

Two factors coincided to take Deacon Blue's performance to a new level. Firstly, securing the contract was a great relief to the band, and transformed them into a confident unit, certain of their own ability. The second factor was the advent of Lorraine McIntosh who not only lit up the songs with her highly distinctive voice, meshing beautifully with Ross', but was also a frenetic and exciting presence on stage, illuminating their entire set. Deacon Blue now had a licence to be themselves and, since Ross' muse was often celebratory, those shows around the turn of the year were incendiary. Ross remembered that, 'You're only out there for forty minutes, so fuck it, go for it.'

Ross had been waiting for this chance long enough for his head not to be turned by the prospect of a little cash coming his way. His colleagues in the band had also been around the music industry for a while – now in their late twenties, they weren't about to let this chance slip. In between gigs, there was time for some serious thinking about what their approach would be in the next year. 'We learned a lot,' noted Ross. 'We're not the kind of band who say, "We've got a record contract, so we'll give it six months, get smashed out your brains every night and have a really good time." That's not the kind of group it is.'

The entirely logical and mature attitude might have upset the press with its insatiable appetite for good stories but it served the band well. Its only downside was that Ross was increasingly portrayed as a hard-headed careerist with his eyes fixed on the main chance, uninterested in the finer points of music and only out to make a quick buck. Later pronouncements tended to back up that impression, for as he revealed to *Vox* in 1994, 'Over the course of Deacon Blue coming together, I abandoned any strong views of what sort of band I wanted to be in and rather let it take its course. Hence the fairly ad hoc nature of the formation.' Ross was well enough versed in the workings of popular culture not to make a rod for his own back by making such thoughts public back in 1986, but such reticence didn't in the end alleviate the pressure on the band, the press making their views very clear. But Ross and Deacon Blue knew where they'd come from, were steeped in the music that mattered to them and were totally unconcerned about any such criticisms that might be abroad.

Ross had a thoroughly clear-eyed view of what he was aiming for and a plan of attack that would enable him to achieve his goals. But *Melody Maker* sounded a warning note: 'Sometimes you can catch a whiff of arrogance about Deacon Blue, the scent of the wide blue CBS yonder already in their nostrils. Self belief or self deceit?'

Deacon Blue were never the kind of group that needed to set out in manifestos what they were about *à la* Dexy's Midnight Runners or the Style Council. However, Ross was happy to explain just what kind of group they were, almost as an attempt to quell the bandwagon of expectation that was already beginning to run away with the group. He was forced to admit later that, 'There's a terrible tendency towards hyperbole from critics . . . and that's what always worried me the most, even before we had anything released; the sycophantic, Great White Hope school of criticism.' Build 'em up and knock 'em down.

Live audiences caught a glimpse of just what the band were looking for and the wide variety of influences they were casting into the melting pot in their choice of covers which included Dylan's 'Like A Rolling Stone' – Ross' favourite song – Van Morrison's 'Angeliou' and Hüsker Dü's 'It's Not Funny Anymore', a fairly mixed bag. The aspirations were not just Ross' but those of the whole group. 'I think there's a desire to want everything . . . at points wanting to be the Rolling Stones, at points wanting to be Bobby Womack, at others wanting to be Gram Parsons or Funkadelic or something . . . we'll never be any of those things but that's probably the most ambitious thing about the band, just to try and get all those things that we love.'

Many commentators found that such admissions indicated delusions of grandeur within the Deacon Blue camp while others found such simple plain speaking to be engaging and refreshing, a nice change from the many groups who pretend to have arrived from outer space without any discernible influences, when they're clearly cribbing material from an assortment of antecedents. If anything, Graeme Kelling was even more straightforward. 'Sure we steal. Who bloody doesn't? Call it eclecticism, call it plagiarism, call it whatever you want. It still comes back to the same thing. There's guitar riffs that have been played a million times over with different kinds of guitars in a different series but they're still the same guitar riffs. I see nothing wrong with lifting ideas at all.'

Having let off steam with a series of concerts at the tail-end of the year, 1987 dawned with the group getting ready to enter the recording studio to come up with their first single and a debut album that would justify CBS's faith and investment in them. Inevitably it was a situation which exerted some pressure on them, particularly Ross since it was his songs that would make or break the group, but they approached the sessions with a fairly relaxed air.

Recording, after all, was one of the reasons that each had found themselves in Deacon Blue, though prior to entering the studio, it was sensible to re-examine and re-state their reasons for being in a group. Ross remained steadfast: '[we are] a rock band. It's important that we come clean about that. When I first started writing songs, I was quite influenced by the anti-rock attitudes of people like Scritti Politti. I thought being in a band was just one big cliché and I wanted simply to be a songwriter and work with session musicians and a producer. But if you destroy the band ethic completely, you actually end up destroying a lot of the good things about music.'

By now in full flow, he went on to expand the hopes he had for Deacon Blue more fully to Adrian Thrills. 'Over the past few years, rock has been a dirty word and I can see why. A lot of rock attitudes are mundane and reactionary and a lot of rock lyrics just reaffirm redundant ideas about sexuality. That's why so many people have thrown away their leather jackets to be in soul bands. But there are still a lot of good things in rock music.' Having talked a good game, the time was ready for Ricky Ross to finally put those plans into action.

CHAPTER FIVE

What was it that drew Muff Winwood and Gordon Charlton of CBS into the world of Deacon Blue? What exactly did they see in this new group from Glasgow that persuaded them to part with large chunks of corporate money? By this stage, the press had given them all the support they required, pumping up their ability as a live act and Ross' unquestioned talent as both singer and songwriter. Yet only CBS had the presence of mind to sign up the group.

As a songwriter, Ross was unrivalled at the head of the new Glaswegian pack. His songs had that added element, however, a dramatic sense which built throughout to an inevitably climactic conclusion. In addition, he was writing in a very literate manner yet without condescension, speaking in a very direct way to an audience who, if they could not always relate to the specifics in the songs, could readily understand and empathize with the emotional weight that he was exposing.

As a politically aware character in the widest sense of the term, Ross would often draw on situations that surrounded him, embroidering them, lighting them in such a way as to expose the human drama that could unfold. 'You draw on your own personal way of seeing things and try and make some kind of common humanity out of it,' he explained. 'Tom Waits and *Frank's Wild Years* – if you look at that, as so much American art, music, drama, film, it draws on distorted American minds, on stories which are so fantastic on one level you can't relate . . . Cagney, "Look Ma, I'm on top of the world" – these quirky, distorted characters have become so much part of our culture that we can relate to bits of them.'

Ross' greatest strength as a writer was in trapping everyday pieces of life and weaving them into some greater picture. At the same time, the smooth contours of the music, the soulful rock fusion that the band operated within, made Deacon Blue look a very good bet for the stadium circuit. Ross was stoically unmoved by the idea, not pretending to despise the prospect as many up and coming rockers would, yet not feverish with anticipation either. 'One or two people have said we're very stadium orientated. I suppose that's not a bad thing if you can do something good with it.' Never one to shirk a challenge, Ross was not a man to view the term 'stadium rock' with the same jaundiced eye as many others. If success took Deacon Blue into those arenas, he would simply ensure that the group gave the best possible account of themselves they could. If they didn't reach that plateau of success, Ross would be content to simply make good records.

This highly open-minded attitude to the rock business was unusual, to say the least, if only because it tended to destroy his credibility in the eyes of professional observers. From a record company perspective, however, Ross' determination to work within the industry's parameters was both refreshing and very alluring, since it suggested that Deacon Blue would be able to play for very large stakes indeed. Even the supporters of the group remarked upon their utterly traditional attitude to the rock machinery and to their music, though Ross' feminist romanticism and determination to write from a female as well as a male perspective gave things a twist.

There's no reason why every or indeed any group that arrives on the scene has to try to be revolutionary and wholly original. No such animal exists though this is rarely admitted in the business circles. For good solid marketing reasons, though, it's useful to formulate new fashions in music to keep people interested in the medium. What the companies really like, however, is an artist that comes along, sticks with the tried and tested and does it professionally. Deacon Blue with their desire to bring together the best of traditional white rock melody and the most exciting soul rhythms, and with their undoubted musical ability must have struck CBS as an answer to their prayers.

CBS were not dealing with snotty young kids who thought they knew everything about making records, but an intelligent, thoughtful, mature act who were more than willing to learn while capable of making their own constructive suggestions. Initially fears might have been aroused when Ross went on the record prior to signing with his worries about engaging in company politics: 'I don't really want to be involved in this business at all. I always thought we needed a deal with a major record company but recently, since I've been meeting some of them, I've just got nothing in common with them at all. You ask, "Do I want to trust somebody like that?" I was reading that magazine I hate to read, *Music Week*. All these business guys theorizing about music and every single bit of it was geared to them succeeding. The guy from the BBC saying, "We want the BBC to nurture established acts, we want the record companies to promote fewer new acts and establish long-term acts."'

Yet for every denouncement of the record companies, Ross would paradoxically link himself to the goal of success, both artistic and commercial. 'I think if someone's going to say to you, you can't be honest, you can't be politically honest, you can't be socially honest, you can't be lyrically honest if you're old or you're with a major record company or whatever, that's ridiculous. It negates all the things I like about music.'

Once the group began work on their first CBS recordings, however, such peripheral worries were pushed to one side to be dealt with later. The confidence that CBS had in them was amply borne out by the choice of producer, the highly respected Jon Kelly whose most notable previous work had been with Kate Bush. Unlike his work with her, the Deacon Blue sessions progressed very quickly, possibly with one eye paying close attention to the budget. Although CBS had apparently underwritten Deacon Blue to the highly melodious tune of £75,000, promotion and live expenses were to be taken into account and so there was no opportunity for recording excess. Not that the band needed too much time, confident and familiar as they were with the material they were to record.

That they should be put straight into the studio was a welcome vote of confidence from the CBS executives and the group determined to repay that faith, utilizing their enthusiasm for playing live to add spontaneity to the recording process, Ross saying, 'We even took time out to go and play live when we were recording. That might be a very old-fashioned idea, but it was one that we learned from. You pick up little ad-libs and improvisations that become a part of the songs in the studio. It stops things from becoming too sterile.'

As good as his word, Ross had clearly studied his record collection well and attempted to introduce the cohesive structure of an *Abbey Road*, of which he had spoken so warmly, into his own recording. *Raintown* was not by any stretch of the imagination a return to the dreaded territory of the concept album, but it did busy itself around recurring themes, with Glasgow, or a town very much like it, being the focus of attention.

Ross conceded the reference point, admitting, 'I always seem to have a love-hate relationship with the town I'm living in. I had it in Dundee and now I've got it in Glasgow. I get really annoyed with my home town when I'm there and then I really miss it when I'm away. I suppose the idea of *Raintown* is based on Glasgow. For a start, it is always raining there. It's to do with my ambivalence about Glasgow. It can be the best place in the world, but sometimes it can also drag you down, stopping you from seeing anything beyond it.'

Raintown was an album characterized by its intelligent wordiness, though it had little of that mysticism that Ross found so inspiring in Mike Scott. '[He] makes perfect sense. I know there's something there and when he sings sometimes like "that hideous strength" there's a whole lot more meaning in that . . . he's possibly the most powerful lyricist around at the moment and the most underrated.' Ross in contrast was a little more explanatory. The flagship song on *Raintown* was 'Dignity', a song which *Melody Maker* had described as being, 'About politics, pride, but most of all, people and it's emotional enough to bring tears to [Norman] Tebbitt's eyes.' A little excessive possibly, but indicative of Ross' stance.

Politics was high on Ross' agenda but his view of the political landscape was not simply one of left and right, or of a musical version of doctrinal argument. Ross wanted to look at the impact of political philosophy on real lives. An avowed socialist, Ross could not help but be angry at the way in which Glasgow, like most industrial centres in the United Kingdom, had been run down. Yet 'Dignity' set the whole political question in a completely different context. The metaphor was slightly laboured, perhaps, a council workman cleaning the streets but saving up his money to sail off into the sunset on a dinghy he was going to buy and call 'Dignity' but the song made its point about both the need to find dignity in work and the numbingly negative effects of that search.

Recalling his own days as a working man, 'Teaching . . . got me thinking about the sheer drudgery of those who have to do the really shitty jobs. There must be about seventy per cent of the people working in this country who simply detest their jobs. That must be an awful position to be in. So I feel quite ambivalent about the work ethic. It's one thing saying that everyone should have a job, but when that job involves simply trying to fight to escape the drudgery, I begin to wonder if that kind of work is actually all that desirable. But "Dignity" is not a message song. It's deliberately ambivalent. It's up to people to make their own minds up about it.'

That final disclaimer was relevant, indeed essential, for if 'Dignity' showed anything, it was that its creator was himself uncertain of just what the political future should look like at its most desirable. As one presenting himself as a thoughtful artist who had an interest in the life of the nation, he was turning himself into a sitting target.

He further explained 'Dignity', suggesting that it was 'a song about work, not unemployment. One of the things that people have been talking about for a long time now is this thing called the right to work . . . but I don't think many people have thought through just what that implies . . . There's just been a feeling for a long time that it would be good if we could have full employment. Every liberal person that I know – myself included – has gone along with that. And when you stop to think about it, think about someone doing some job in some place, you can't think of any job you've done that you'd like to be in. And the whole idea of the dignity of labour seems to me to be a dubious one . . . [Some people have] a terrible job that could have been done by a machine . . . is that what everybody wants? Is that what all the fuss is about? Because if that's what it means to be unemployed, is that any better? Sure, it may be better money and yes, of course, there is some dignity in providing for yourself and your family. But that can't be all there is.'

There is some substance to these comments insofar as people would prefer exciting, interesting careers with the potential to achieve personal fulfilment. Quite clearly there is something to be said about constructing an economy where the drudgery is removed. Nonetheless, many jobs that most might consider unpleasant need to be done – street cleaning, sewage work, working long, unsociable hours in menial jobs within the electricity industry or in the health service. Many of these kinds of manual jobs cannot, for the foreseeable future at least, be done by machines.

For many, many people, getting a job of any sort is all that they can worry about for it is this that puts a roof over their heads, feeds and clothes the children, etc. In suggesting that a job might not be the universal panacea that we should all be striving for, Ross may have a point. But it's a point that is only applicable to a successful society with adequate welfare provisions and a thriving economy. The loss of the work ethic would be of far greater consequence than Ross seems to imply or comprehend. The concept of having gainful and useful employment has been the cornerstone on which the social fabric of the country has been built. Ross of all people with his background in youth clubs should have appreciated the link between teenage unemployment and crime. His solution, beautiful, ambitious and romantic as it might be, was also a recipe for serious social unrest. Remember Toxteth '81, Ricky?

By definition almost, it was written that Ross and Deacon Blue had to aspire, had to be escapist and ambitious. A song such as 'Dignity' was all about one individual accumulating his savings so that he could escape a life of drudgery. It did not deal with the years of miserable toil, salting away a few pennies every week until that final chance of escape might become a reality. It did not address the issue that thousands, probably millions in a nation without a minimum wage structure would never be able, no matter how carefully they shepherded their resources, to save sufficient money to escape the workplace. It ignored the fact that many people are required to work above and beyond the age of retirement simply to make ends meet in times of inadequate state pensions. Yet by simply wanting it, by wishing hard enough, magically we could all acquire our own ship called 'Dignity' and all would be well. The tears that *Melody Maker* suggested would be brought to Tebbitt's eyes would have been ones of relief at the naivety of another caring pop star wearing his heart on his sleeve. Ross was clearly capable of much better than this.

In the inane consumerist eighties, Ross stood out from the pop crowd by virtue of his commitment and earnest political beliefs; in no sense are we questioning his devotion to socialist principles, merely questioning the way in which he applied them musically. Unfortunately for Ross, he was unable to dismiss 'Dignity' as 'just another pop song to entertain people'. He'd already nailed his colours very firmly to the mast; Ross was a musician who, we were told, was trying to make a difference.

His method, by reflecting on human nature and frailties and realistic situations, spoke volumes about his personal warmth and the engaging and very genuine concern he had for people and their situations. However, it refused to acknowledge that at their root, political questions need political rather than personal solutions.

'Dignity', in keeping with other sections of the *Raintown* album, seemed like an attempt to say something in political terms about the predicament of working people. There seems little question that Ross was sensitive to jibes that he was just another bleeding heart, shedding crocodile tears about the awful plight of some of his fellow Glaswegians while filling his pockets with money earned from a capitalist industry. Brian Eno has spoken about music being an exciting medium since it is that place where art and commerce meet, but this seems a delusory comment, for precious little artistic merit is placed before commercial necessity these days, with the exception of already well-established acts such as those with whom Eno works.

Ross was sailing his own ship from the dreary workaday world by virtue of his talents as a singer and songwriter. As such, he represents all the virtues of a free market capitalist system – people want to share in the fruits of his talent, placing his records in their lives, either as treasured possessions or simply background sound. Whatever the reason, Ross still gets paid and under a government with a commitment to what it euphemistically terms 'wealth creation' – i.e. allowing the wealthy to create more money – he was likely to have a very comfortable existence, aided by particularly advantageous rates of income tax. As U2 have said, perhaps his role should be to bite the hand that feeds him, but Ross has never been as radically engaged as that. By 1991, *Q* were to describe him as 'too polite and reasonable to be great'.

A harsh assessment possibly in the light of some of his songs, but it was that reasonableness, described by some as maturity, that forced Ross to consider his position around *Raintown* and what it might become if the record was the success that everyone anticipated it would be. '*Raintown* will be the only LP like this, but it had to be like this. When I first met Graeme I said to him, "What have you been doing till now?" and he said, "Oh, this and that, trying to get out of here mainly." I said, "I've been trying to do that for the last three years and I haven't had much joy."'

Such comments are a double-edged sword for Ross. On the one hand, they suggest that his uplifting songs of hope and dreams are honest reflections of his own desire to improve his lot and achieve and improve upon the security that his father had before him. At the same time though, they make Deacon Blue appear to be no more than a simple form of escape, a means to an end. Taken at face value, these comments portray Ross as hard-headed, playing a style of music which he had selected as being the most likely route to the big bucks.

It can't be stressed too strongly in the light of these comments that Ross does appear to be genuinely in love with his music. It seems clear too that he wanted to make his songs as popular as possible not purely for his own benefit and that of the group but also to get some kind of message across, even if that was as vague as generalized sympathy and understanding of the intense boredom experienced by someone working on the production line somewhere.

One problem of which Ross was acutely aware and which that quote does touch upon was that, as someone commenting on Glasgow and its problems – though never attempting to be the spokesman for the city or for Scotland – he had limited time to do so. Scottish problems were largely created by right-wing politics and so the Scots in general were demanding left-wing solutions. Ross himself was a firm believer in the need for change, but as a man coming from the left, success would inevitably hamper his ability to demand that change.

Ross, like fellow Glaswegians, wanted a means of escaping the nine-to-five and his financial penury. While unemployed, as he was for some time, he had credibility in demanding solidarity in order to implement socialist solutions. Once his star was in the ascendant, however, as he began to sell records, he would of necessity leave his contemporaries behind; that is not to say that he would turn his back on friendships, nor that he would not help worthwhile causes that were important to him. However, he would be moving in very different financial circles. While Ross' ideals might remain intact, many others find that the influx of cash is more important to them; just look at how many people have shifted in their allegiance from Labour or Liberal to Conservative in the wake of tax bribes. As a person's lot improves, priorities change and ideology can change with them.

It takes a major effort of will to hold on to ideals that might harm you financially while benefiting those worse off. There is no evidence to suggest that Ross has sacrificed any of his political beliefs in the pursuit of success, nor that that success has in any way changed those ideals. What it does change is people's perception of him. For *Raintown*, he was identified as a voice of his city, recognition that Ross would never have claimed for himself. Once that record had sold, though, he was that rich so-and-so who had a hit record. Why is he talking about unemployment? Champagne socialist.

To give him his due, Ross understood the difficulty he would face which is part of the reason that *Raintown* turned out as it did, a celebration of ordinary people's lives and their everyday struggles, while Ross could still claim an understanding of them without being shouted down. He anticipated the turning of the tide in 'Loaded' which was an attack on the corruption of values by the invidious influence of money. Ross confessed, 'I always find it strange when the designer socialists in London start sounding off about the plight of the working classes. I'm not saying that they don't care, but a lot of the time they are the ones who have an active investment in the current state of the nation. It just seems hypocritical hearing a lecture from someone who is very much part of the successful side of Britain. What I'm saying is that it is actually different for those who are at the bottom of the pile.' And those who sell platinum quantities of albums represent the successful side; Ross did not have any intention of becoming a hypocrite and so this was almost his only chance to sound off at a decade of injustice.

Ross was quite correct about things being different at the bottom, and this was where 'Dignity' held its own. At the bottom, no one cares about socialist or capitalist arguments, but about concepts more central to their lives like home, faith, work – the pull of your hometown was a theme that recurred on *Raintown*, the album and the song, as Ross' conflicting feelings tore at him. What it did give him was a sense of perspective on life at the bottom of the heap. Life there is far more clear-cut, it is simply about getting off the bottom, trying to pull yourself up by whatever means necessary. If you do succeed, why not relish the financial rewards? Why worry about political ideals? These are the currently insoluble problems that the left has to tackle. Without arriving at some viable answers, they will not change the face of the nation, something which Ross was keen to see happen.

As a lyricist, this was solid territory for Ross and his bitter attack on those flaunting their wealth in celebration of the supposed late-eighties boom – though does anyone out there who isn't an estate agent actually remember seeing any of the beneficial effects of this alleged boom? – while simultaneously wringing their hands at the parlous situation in which the downtrodden masses found themselves, a situation created deliberately to foster the financial health of an elite minority. As far as 'Loaded' went, Ross noted that it was about 'money. I always try to say something in my songs – what's the point in doing it otherwise?' With 'Loaded', a human story with a wider application, he succeeded where 'Dignity' had failed.

Interestingly, these were the first two singles which CBS released from *Raintown* and neither made an impression on the charts. In their initial incarnations, both were probably too restrained for the mass market especially as they were offerings from an unknown band. Musically, they were intriguing, 'Loaded' boasting a glorious melody, an effervescent vocal performance coloured with a particularly human and therefore affecting moment when Ross' voice broke into a laugh, supported by a chorus which screamed 'hit', but both elements were a trifle understated, working best in the context of the parent album.

What else can be made of *Raintown*. Fortunately, for most of its sprawl, Ross absorbed himself in human emotion drawn out by situations rather than situations glibly portrayed as universal answers. The opening trilogy of songs, 'Born in a Storm', 'Raintown' and 'Ragman' were a stunning statement of intent, beautiful, stately songwriting that would have graced any era, yet was highly contemporary.

'Born in a Storm' was the ideal opener, a piano tinkling in the background as Ross crooned away like he was sitting on a barstool at three in the morning next to Frank Sinatra. It effortlessly captured a sense of place, and its very own atmosphere of defeat, dejection and defiance. Rolling straight in to 'Raintown' and then on into 'Ragman', images of dislocation, separation, ambition and yearning followed. Given that Ross and his wife Zara were weathering the final storm in their marriage at this stage, it's tempting as with all artists to cast the shadow of autobiography over the work – certainly the protagonist in this song was a man with an eye on his destiny, waiting for a call to turn his life around while his partner was unimpressed by these empty dreams and divorced from the life he hoped to lead, the 'raintown' metaphor extending to this separation as well as the drab environment of a dead-end city that crushes dreams and yet remains home. The two songs in tandem shouted out very clearly that you do not have to be held back by your surroundings and environment and that there are ways to escape if you have faith in yourself. 'Raintown' also seemed to speak of the power of music, the way in which favourite records on the radio can be like old friends, breathing life into the day, the song itself constantly, restlessly building to a climax.

'Ragman' too was a song for the broken-hearted, dancing

carefully around the disabling power of love, a facet of relationships that's not often touched upon as Ross suggested to *Melody Maker*. 'There is a morality about men/women relationships which doesn't get spoken about very much. I don't hear it from any other songwriters apart from what we do.' Forced into a corner, he later admitted that 'Raintown' was in part a rumination on his personal circumstances. 'Those songs were written during a particularly difficult time in my life and I was feeling trapped in my personal situation. At that time, I thought things were never going to change, that I'd never get away from this place.'

These opening songs gave the new listener a thumb-nail sketch of the range of skills that Deacon Blue would be unleashing on their albums in the future. The musical backing was sympathetic to Ross' intentions with James Prime cleverly inverting the 'Singing in the Rain' Broadwayesque cliché of piano raindrops, to suit the atmosphere set up by 'Born in a Storm', taking it into the highly contemporary sound of 'Raintown' which itself included several of what were virtually John Martyn's trademark synth parts, the product of Prime's previous experience. His rollicking piano work on 'Ragman' was equally stirring, propelling the song along against a strong rhythm section, trading the lead role with Kelling's guitar. However, the most startling instrument on show was Lorraine McIntosh's voice which appeared from nowhere on that song, lighting it up and exaggerating the frustrated growl with which Ross was chewing his way through parts of the song.

Ross is a self-confessed believer in the love song: much of *Raintown* was steeped in the traditions of that form and was unashamedly romantic in tone. And yet for the characters in the songs, things rarely turned out as they would want; the record was filled with misunderstandings, with the fear of commitment, the desire for salvation in the arms of another.

If Ross was talking from personal experience at times, then he wasn't one to spare his own feelings, or those of the people around him. 'Chocolate Girl' was a case in point and a perfect example of the feminist slant to his lyrics, part of his attempt to tear up the tired old language and sexual stereotypes of rock lore and replace them with a vocabulary that could articulate a more modern approach to relationships. 'Chocolate Girl' discussed a typically male case of emotional repression; running through the rituals of courtship by rote, never stopping to actually feel an emotion lest it might be painful or discomforting in some way. Treating his women as just objects, not wondering about their emotions, this character hops in and out of brief relationships with women, each lasting only as long as he chooses.

In exposing fairly standard laddishness, Ross was opening himself up to attack from that contingent, yet it was this unusual vulnerability that made the song so appealing, particularly to the female section of the audience who could believe that Ross understood what it was they wanted from a relationship. Lorraine McIntosh expanded on that to *Melody Maker* when she was tackled on the subject of pornography. 'I've never understood people who're into pornography. I think that's something of a fundamental difference between men and women. I couldn't read a porno mag and find it stimulating simply because the things I find stimulating aren't captured in a photograph – even of someone I love. Their sex is them, being with them as a whole person.'

This enlightened view informed most of Ross' lyrics on the record, victims being portrayed as members of either sex, as oppposed to the simplistic treatment that rock usually meted out in such songs – in standard rock mythology, 'Chocolate Girl' would have been a cause for celebration as 'our hero' successfully had a wonderful time, and don't you wish you were there? In the hands of Deacon Blue, the treatment was sensitive without wallowing in sentimentality and as such thoroughly successful.

'When Will You (Make My Telephone Ring)' was a close relative of 'Chocolate Girl', but distinctive in that this time, Ross was the loser, waiting, dejected, by the phone that never rings. Cursing his wasted time, the exhausted singer cannot bring himself to put the past behind him in a song which *Record*

Mirror termed 'uncannily female in sentiment', putting this down to the fact that Ross is 'evidently a die-hard romantic'. It was true, we've heard this song a hundred times before in the capable hands of innumerable female torch singers, but to hear Ross having to admit to such rejection was a fresh twist and a successful one. Backed by a sumptuous soulful swing, with sonorous backing vocals that gave the track the authentic feel of some Stax classic, 'When Will You (Make My Telephone Ring)' was also to serve as a future blueprint for fellow Glaswegians Wet Wet Wet.

The consequences of love, the way in which it can be destroyed by the fear of being swallowed by its strength, were documented in 'Love's Great Fears', a song seemingly aimed at forcing a last-ditch reconciliation between estranged partners. It provided a nice glimpse of Deacon Blue's strengths, featuring an enormous chorus constructed around a sly guitar figure that was kept low in the mix, yet which was the song's centrepiece. The guitar returned with a yearning solo that neatly summed up Ross' words.

That love is not simply a rosy path, a passport to a wonderful future was illustrated by 'The Very Thing', a song which was used as the theme to the BBC production *Take Me Home*. It coupled together the twin strains of romance and the need to find work to build a future life and as such was a very effective condemnation of the spectre of unemployment, at the same time looking at the fact that it's so difficult to break free from your roots and past experiences. Ross reflected on how love might be portrayed as the greatest means of escape from a grim situation but the harsh realities of life reinforced by personal experience suggested that nothing could be quite as simple as that. Musically it was characterized again by a huge chorus, a country-style guitar from Kelling that somehow fused itself with a different style borrowed from U2's The Edge, while Prime entertained himself with some piano playing that was reminiscent of Van Morrison. This melded to create a rousing, hopeful backing track that was at odds with the darker sentiments of the lyric and therefore worked supremely well.

The album closed with 'A Town to be Blamed', a more sombre exercise that harked back to 'Born in a Storm' and the luck of the luckless. It was a reflection on the importance of roots, the strength that you can draw from your own environment even if at times that environment seems to be holding you back because of its supposed absence of opportunities. As the closer of what was very likely to be a major album, it was also Ross and the band saying goodbye to their previous lives having made good their escape, while sparing a thought for those not as fortunate or determined, those who had not made the leap. It was also an example of self-chastisement, Ross' aspirational zeal telling him that simply by working just a little harder, his dreams might come true.

'A year ago,' he told *Melody Maker* in July 1987, 'we were writing songs till we were blue in the face but never playing. The final track on the LP, "A Town to be Blamed", was the last song I wrote at that time and it's like how, when you look around and you see all the reasons that you're not doing well, it's as fatuous to blame the town you live in as it is to blame anything else. But there are people leaving Glasgow tonight as we speak, on buses and trains just 'cos they want out – just to get nowhere – just to wander up and down Charing Cross Road and stay in that Shelter place.'

'Raintown' was an intimate record, its universality and lack of posturing being the abiding source of its beguiling power. One song that stood apart from the 'small town' feel, though, was 'He Looks Like Spencer Tracy Now', a track which looked kindly on Harold Agnew, a man who had taken illegal photographs of Enola Gay and the aftermath of the Hiroshima bombing. This was a remarkable exposition of Ross' songwriting technique; his compassionate approach to the Jekyll and Hyde character of Agnew that didn't wallow in mawkishness did him proud. He avoided judgemental condemnation for a more studied and realistic approach, verging on 'there but for the Grace of God go I'.

Agnew was harshly treated by the press in the aftermath of his photographs, the hacks venting their spleen on this 'monster'. Ross was not one to excuse Agnew for taking these photographs and profiting from them, but at the same time, he accepted that he was only human after all, that everyone has their frailties, that everyone at some time might be induced to cross the fine line that separates right from wrong.

Part of the target of 'He Looks Like Spencer Tracy Now' was public hypocrisy. Had Agnew's photographs not been published by those that lined up to condemn him, there would have been no story. Allied to that, if Agnew had not taken them, it would have been someone else's job to do so.

The hypocrisy here was that in reality it was what the photographs showed that people could not stomach, not that the photographs had been taken. Until Hiroshima and Nagasaki had been destroyed, no one, certainly not the public at large, really knew quite what devastation would be wrought by the bomb. Until they saw photographs, the full horror of the tragedy was not brought home to people. Agnew was reviled for taking those pictures in just the same way as Oppenheimer was reviled for his part in the creation of the bomb, yet these were men carrying out their work, albeit illegally in Agnew's case.

The use of the bomb was not condoned in the song, nor was it directly condemned. But by treating its impact on one human life, a man on the periphery of it all in one way, it was a most convincing argument against the use of nuclear weapons, an argument that would be most soundly supported by those who actually served in the War and lost friends and colleagues. With 'He Looks Like Spencer Tracy Now', Ross proved himself beyond doubt to be a highly skilled songwriter, capable of capturing a gamut of conflicting emotions within the conventional popular song format. Many had previously danced around the nuclear debate in song, but in widening the focus to look at our own hypocrisy, the impact on all our lives, Ross clearly stated that we should always use every means at our disposal to avoid war, particularly since the stakes are now so high for humanity as a whole.

That, then, was *Raintown*, an album by a new group ready to be despatched to the shops for May release. Deacon Blue were justifiably confident about its contents, happy that they had collectively created a strong body of songs that worked well together and which would be capable of moving people as well as entertaining them royally. What, though, would the press and the public make of it all?

CHAPTER SIX

Although they had used gigs to refresh themselves away from the claustrophobic atmosphere of the studio while recording *Raintown*, Deacon Blue were still relatively inexperienced as far as the live circuit was concerned. Nineteen-eighty-seven was to change all of that as CBS set them on the road to learn what might prove to be the most important aspect of their trade, that of charming a live audience.

Enthusiasm was slightly dampened by the commercial failure of 'Dignity' in March, but the critical plaudits that it garnered seemed to bode well for the future and so the prospect of playing to new audiences was one that, initially at least, seemed enticing. 'The way we approached shows then was almost cathartic . . . we're happy to go along and fit in with whatever's happening and the great thing about that is that every gig's different!' according to Ross, and there was no reason why they shouldn't have enjoyed themselves. After all, this was the culmination of years spent trying to get a group off the ground; to be able to turn professional and write songs for a living.

In their native Glasgow, Deacon Blue had been able to create a reputation of being a fine live group based on the passionate nature of their performance, throwing everything into each show. It was a policy that won them many admirers and explains, in part, the way in which many became devoted followers of the group. The catharsis of the gigs wasn't only restricted to the members of the band, it seemed. They quickly won good reviews, with *Record Mirror*'s verdict on a Marquee show being reasonably typical: 'Passion is another Deacon Blue attribute,' wrote Lesley O'Toole. 'A profound passion strictly not to be confused with that fulsome brand peddled by the likes of Big Country. We are talking gut emotion here.'

Accusations were levied at Ross in particular that he was trying too hard to emulate Springsteen, that he was not sufficiently relaxed to allow his own personality to come through but these were among the few carping comments. While they were on the road to support the release of 'Dignity', *Raintown* reached the shops and the review columns of the press. It received a mixed bag of reviews, some ecstatic, others less so. Len Brown of *New Musical Express* grudgingly accepted that 'as sure as beanz is beanz, it'll be Ricky Ross: Rock Star . . . *Raintown* is a largely unsurprising, uninspiring affair. Too few risks are taken. I'm wondering where are the promised insights into Glasgow life and why isn't there more of Lorraine McIntosh's voice? Less of a Scottish invasion and more of a border skirmish.'

Brown made some salient points, especially in relation to McIntosh's voice which was used rather sparingly for such a vibrant instrument, though over-familiarity might have dulled her effectiveness. However, the review illustrated that Ross' concerns about being the Great White Hope were well founded. Ross himself had never pretended to be the true voice of Glasgow, although the grim artwork on the sleeve – an impressive photograph, dark and depressing – did suggest that here was a serious work.

If they didn't want to become Glasgow's representatives, neither did Ross or his colleagues suggest that Deacon Blue were anything other than a traditional rock band looking to explore their roots. Deacon Blue had never represented themselves as a fountain of avant-garde originality, but saw themselves more as a safe pair of hands. It was this characteristic that endeared them to their fans and had recommended them to CBS.

As something of a supporter of the group, it was to be expected that *Sounds* might look on them favourably and such was the case, Mat Snow bestowing four of a possible five stars on them. 'Ricky Ross is twenty-nine and acts his age,' wrote Snow. 'He evokes moods and portrays viewpoints which ring true to the life of someone who's lived, observed and pondered a little.' He recommended these 'small dramas of effusive but deft tunefulness . . . these introspective sepia tints of romance and home are symptomatic of how record companies are increasingly pitching to the over twenty-fives,' a perceptive comment which sounded something of a warning to those self-appointed arbiters of taste for whom rock should avoid such intimations of maturity.

Ross was broadly in agreement with these comments, saying, 'It's hard to describe, but there was a lot of me that felt disappointed about growing up and realizing that things become much more complex and difficult and that all the innocence and joy of it all disappears. I've always wanted to write songs that are indicative of that. When you reach the age of twenty-five, you assume that everything will work itself out and it just isn't like that at all.'

The only real criticism that Snow had to make in his review was in terms of the record's production values: 'Do guitars have to roar with that manicured jet engine smoothness?' It was a reasonable question. Nobody could doubt the instrumental proficiency that *Raintown* showcased, for each member of Deacon Blue could be justifiably proud of their contribution to the finished album. Nevertheless, the whole thing did seem over-polished if anything, every note having been carefully thought out and placed cleverly up against its neighbour. There is a certain craftsmanship in that approach which is admirable, but in terms of a rock 'n' roll record, it did leave a slightly anodyne taste in the mouth. Ross had been quoted as saying, 'With Dylan, I like the willingness to change, to move in different directions, to take his own songs, break them down and do something different . . . most of all though, I like the roughness he gets.'

It was a characteristic that had no place on *Raintown*, something which Adam Sweeting, something of a *bête noire* as far as Deacon Blue were concerned in the years to come, picked up on: 'Deacon Blue's album bears the sad stamp of "too much budget, not enough control" right down the middle.' Grudgingly admitting that 'the songwriting suggests potential' Sweeting went on to opine that, '*Raintown* doesn't present a group, it merely suggests that you admire its production values . . . Deacon Blue already sound like middle-aged session men, which can't possibly have been their intention.'

Sweeting's biting critique hinted at a deeper malaise within the Deacon Blue camp. There were few willing to argue with Ross' songwriting talents, even though there were worries at an overly obsessive concern with technique. However, there were suggestions that it was CBS who were not only holding the purse strings but were directing musical operations too. Having admitted to early worries as to just how things would go in the belly of the corporate beast, Ross now had few qualms, telling *Sounds* in July 1987, 'We're very pleased with the way [CBS are] handling things at the moment.'

Further to that, he continued, 'We want them to put out singles that they feel most comfortable with. What's the point in signing to a major record company unless you are going to give them a chance to do their job? That's the way of the world. They are a big record company and they know how to go about the job of getting your record heard by as many people as possible. I don't know anything about selling records. Until I do, I'm not going to go and bang on their table.'

Ross clearly understood that Deacon Blue's elevation to the major league with CBS was not exactly the recipe for winning success within the professionally cynical music press and so he was careful to point out that the relationship with CBS was hunky dory and that, so far as making the music went, Deacon

Blue were completely in control. Hindsight illustrates fairly clearly that Ross wasn't especially interested in what the music press had to say, for he had his sights set on a far broader world beyond those close confines, but he was equally aware that he had to humour them while the group were trying to get off the ground and still only had cult-band status.

'We know we're in a great position,' admitted Ross. 'But I think we have to take a lot of credit for that. Because when you sign to a record label, very few people there know anything about you at all. It's up to you how much impact you have on that label. People assume an awful lot about record companies but they don't really know how they operate. Record labels work exactly the same way a writer [for the music press] works. If they hear a group and they like them, if they work up a degree of enthusiasm for [the group], then they're going to do their best to help them. And that's how it works at record companies.

'But even then,' Ross went on, 'when you've convinced them to give you their best shot, you still have to be prepared to try to push your opinions, to tell them how you want them to work for you. I think that by now they've all got the message that we won't let anything slip by us, because we go in there occasionally and say, "Look, we're not having this and we're not having that!"'

Ross occasionally admitted to a little irritation at the press' insistence that taking the CBS pay cheque meant that their musical message would have to be diluted, an accusation he thoroughly refuted. 'I think the good thing is that no one has made us do anything we don't want to. Okay, we had to take the word "shit" from the original version of "Dignity" but it's that whole extension of what you do and what you want to do. Do we want to make a tape and six people to hear it or do we want to make a record and sell it to millions of people. No one can tell me they're on a major label and they don't want to do the latter thing. We want to reach as many people as possible and meet them.'

There was apparently a high degree of trust between Deacon

Blue and CBS, Ross recalling their decision to sign. 'Our A & R man is high on the list of people we trust. Before he signed us, he quoted the lines of "Dignity". He was pissed, but he got them all right and he knew what they meant.'

Even so, given Ross' ambition, his determination to play the pop game to win and his unabashedly populist stance, suspicions were rife that CBS had merely signed Deacon Blue because they could see the likelihood of healthy sales. Such an argument is of course pointless. It's very unlikely that a major record company would put up the high level of investment necessary to launch a group if it didn't feel that it would be recouped by future sales. It is true that that attitude stifles originality and creativity, militating against new artists that might be something of a risk, but Deacon Blue had never pretended to be that sort of group. *Sounds'* Robin Gibson was closer to the mark, writing, 'It'd be stupid to ask if success will spoil Deacon Blue because success is what they're geared towards.'

Probably the most powerful weapon in Deacon Blue's armoury in the event of having to take a stand against CBS was their maturity. Having played on the fringes of pop for a while, they knew what to expect and they knew a little more about the world at large than a group of teenagers dazzled by the headlights of fame. 'It will be easier for us to cope,' confirmed Ross. 'Our rise has been very gradual. We haven't been thrown in at the deep end.'

Nevertheless, there was some disquiet as Ross and his colleagues made no bones about their desire to achieve massive success, an aspiration not generally admitted to with such undisguised relish. They recognized that roadwork would be the pathway to that success and so they took to it very happily. 'We've been touring almost non-stop since we signed to CBS,' reflected Ross in July. 'First of all we toured to get the band's name known. And then we toured to promote the first single. And now we're touring to promote the album. And whenever we stop gigging we have to get up early to go on the telly!'

Those live dates continued to go down well. Angie Daniell

wrote of their Mean Fiddler show in June that their music was 'a joyous statement, and positively evangelical, considering the effect it had on the audience who so identified with the light he was shining, they almost started speaking in tongues . . . the sort of band who are nice to be with.' A month later, *Sounds* reviewed a Marquee show in similarly encouraging terms: 'Deacon Blue are human . . . totally at ease with their audience with a genuine affection which serves to temper singer Ricky's semi-parodic macho posturing and prevents the band from straying too close to the edge. The Stateside references . . . [tip] more than a sly wink to conventional rock mythology. Believe me, you could do a lot worse.'

By September, Tom Morton was writing that, 'Their strategy for fame and fortune is traditionally rockist – tour and tour and tour until U2 you become. As a live band, they're becoming just ridiculously confident – and effectively so. Lorraine and Ricky are developing a vocal and visual interplay worth lots of new gold dreams and the songs, stately and shapely and dripping emotion, take you apart . . . a fan's band, their day is on the horizon.' While they were starting to win people over, the fact that they were still playing at venues such as the Mean Fiddler in Harlesden did betray that matters were not progressing as quickly as they might.

Early sales of *Raintown* were sluggish and, in the wake of the failure of 'Loaded' to graze the charts, CBS decided that further measures needed to be taken. In America, the 'No Risk Disc' policy was one which was well accepted and a regular means of attracting people unwilling to take a risk on a new artist. The gist of the policy was that CBS made cassette copies of *Raintown* available to a number of shops around Britain and according to their press release, 'This is the first time that a major record company has taken such a positive step to break a new act. It means that the public can purchase a cassette of *Raintown* and in the unlikely event of them not enjoying it, can return it to the shop within a few days and get a full cash refund.

It's a measure of our complete belief in Deacon Blue and our commitment to them.'

If some would applaud this as an imaginative new way of introducing a new act to the public, to others who had observed the music scene for many years, it seemed rather gimmicky – the fact that only selected outlets would receive the offer immediately begged the question as to whether or not these were chart return shops. Whatever the case, it gave the record a useful nudge, pushing sales up to around 10,000 as less than one in twenty purchasers returned the cassette.

Even so, a peak placing of No. 82 in the album charts was not the trail-blazing opening to a meteoric career that many had imagined and on which CBS had banked. A few cynics found it hard to stifle the odd giggle at CBS's failure, and Deacon Blue soon had to get used to being a stick with which the press could beat the major companies.

In fact, at the outset, Deacon Blue and CBS were far from being the machiavellian shysters that others would later suggest; it was naivety that cost them so dear in their early recording career. It was always apparent that they were a band who would grow on people rather than having immediate appeal; for that reason, they might have been better served by releasing one lead-off single well ahead of *Raintown* rather than just a couple of months ahead. With that single available to the public, the band could then have gone on a really extensive tour of the country, building up an audience over six months ready for the LP release. Ironically that would have been evidence of a strategical master plan for the group's future. As it was, they were being criticized for having a level of animal cunning that they had failed to achieve. The 'No Risk Disc' policy was only necessitated by the incompetence with which the album had been launched.

Nineteen-eighty-seven became one long tunnel of concerts for Deacon Blue and by the end of the year there were few more formidable rock acts in the country. They had also succeeded in making the jump in status from clubs to bigger venues. Just prior to Christmas, they played a sold-out show at London's Town and Country Club. Paul Oldfield described their sound for *Melody Maker* as being 'a hothouse FM production in which rock chords, fretted tight funk guitar and the melisma of Lorraine's soul/gospel backing vocals are a perfect laminate, a saturated but high-definition surface. Not a chink of doubt, just the even proportional finish of pop's global consensus.'

Observers were, by the end of the year, falling over themselves to mourn the loss of Deacon Blue's vulnerability, seeing them now as a juggernaut rock band clad in some protective steel sheen. Yet this was obviously not the case as Ross explained. 'We learned our trade on those shows [in 1987]; we used to play student bars where they'd stand twenty-five feet away and your job wasn't to sing but to get them down the front. Some nights were really good. Eventually it came to a very scary stop: I collapsed. We'd been on the road too long, and a lot of other, quite personal things had gone on – I was going through a very difficult period of separation. One night in November '87 in Norwich, I looked round and suddenly felt physically unwell and very vulnerable. I couldn't go back on. So we took a couple of weeks off – and then did some more gigs!'

Live work was a mixed blessing for Deacon Blue through 1987. In spite of the exhausting schedule which had left Ross at such a low ebb physically and mentally they were happy to play live, feeling that it was the best way of reaching a new audience. Most importantly, it also provided them with some of their most touching moments, confirmation that they were in the right business as Ross explained: 'We were caught in this Glasgow traffic-jam when someone rushed over and started tapping on the window. He says, "I just wanted to tell you about that gig you did last night. I got off with this girl and we've . . . well I guess we've sort of fallen in love and my life feels great all of a sudden, like things make sense all of a sudden.' It might not have had much to do with the music or the actual gig, but it was a magical moment. We all sat there and we wanted to cry.'

More disturbing for Deacon Blue as a credible force as purveyors of thoughtful, intelligent pop/rock, were Paul Oldfield's comments on their Town and Country Club concert in December: 'Their upfulness is doctrinal. Deacon Blue have to be seen to be speaking on behalf of all of us, articulating what we want to say . . . they persist in offering the defeated or inarticulate a voice.' The vulnerability that was so attractive on *Raintown* had been lost in the rush to convert punters, Deacon Blue unfortunately slipping back towards the bad habits they'd cultivated when they were so desperate to attract a record company. Oldfield went on, '"This Town To Blame" [*sic*] doesn't succumb to bewilderment about collapsing communities but turns to defiant hope, carnivore US rock. Like Springsteen, any dissent or despair gets lost in the thrust . . . but how much more subversive babble or silences would be than this managed, balanced and impeccably constructed sound.'

This was something that Ross railed against, for it was central to his songwriting philosophy that things should go beyond the surface in his songs. 'I always found it frustrating that people tend to see songs within these narrow confines. Someone said to me recently that the reason our photographs are smudged on our record sleeve is because we're trying to distance ourselves as people. In a way it is. Being a pop figure gets in the way of the song. I want people to accept the songs as their own and not as the working out of my back pages.

'My songs,' he continued, 'I hope always leave a door open for someone to come in. If you close that door and give them something with no imagination or irony required, no other avenues you can bring to it, then you may as well watch a TV show or a film which will continue running whether you're there or not. The live show is the same thing; it's communal, a contract between us and the audience.'

However, this desire to remove his personality from the songs meant that those less well disposed to the band could portray them as faceless, lacking in any personality, and consequently ideal as an undemanding night out for those not wishing to think too hard. This was rather unfair, for Ross had lost none of his desire to inform as well as entertain, gaining a reputation for haranguing the audience in the run-up to the 1987 election. 'I was doing a lot of that stuff up until the election 'cos it was a focus for people. Obviously I don't want people to think that if they go and see Deacon Blue they're gonna get shouted at. I just thought the night before the election at the Town and Country Club was as far as I could go. Why not – if it's in a good cause, anything goes.'

That politics still got under Ross' skin was clear in the aftermath of the disappointing election result when Deacon Blue were booked to play at the Cambridge Ball and their audience were not in sympathy with his views. 'I suppose I took a bit of a bad mood at it. I couldn't cope with it all and, by the end, I just said something like, "Here's one for all you greedy bastards who are gonna have to sell your British Telecom shares." The audience was so drunk I don't think they noticed.' One of the ironies of all this was of course that Deacon Blue were soon to be perceived as the face of CD rock, the CD at that stage being the preserve of the yuppie crowd.

Ross was still unsure of how exactly he should apply his principles. It was important to him that his songs embraced topics that meant something to him. 'This is the feeling in Glasgow, this idea that we're far too earnest for our own good,' said Ross when trying to confront the issue. 'Maybe that's not hip enough? Well, that annoys me and I think it's a stupid outlook. I like sincerity and obviously the ephemeral, trendy fashion scenes are opposed to that value. They want to follow things that are "happening". Values are far down the list. Of course we value words like "faith" and "dignity". I had a very strong religious upbringing and I like a lot of religious words. I use these words very naturally because they're part of my upbringing.'

The virtues of *Raintown* included its powerful choruses, huge swirling moments that sucked an audience in. For many it was a very short step from this to turning themselves into purveyors of what was tagged at the time 'The Big Music' *à la* Simple Minds. CBS certainly were in sympathy with that belief, for it was this that led to the final breakthrough for Deacon Blue, once the services of the inestimable Bob Clearmountain had been engaged.

CHAPTER SEVEN

Ricky Ross had already sorted out an escape route of sorts for himself when he noted that 'you mustn't be too precious about your own songs.' We've already noted his views on Dylan's deconstructionist ethos and so the fact that Ross and Deacon Blue were willing to tamper with their own canon should have come as no surprise. Indeed, given their intensive schedule and the fact that they were beginning to embark on unusually lengthy shows for a group so short on recorded work, it was imperative for their own sanity that they included room for improvisation within their sets.

Of course, changing songs around in live performance is one thing, but rerecording them in search of greater success is something entirely different again. But this was the proposition put to them by an increasingly concerned CBS, worried at the band's surprising inability to take the charts by storm. Reflecting the starker simplicity that the band had introduced to live performance where some of the complex subtleties had been removed from many of the songs – a function of playing to initially uninterested and then highly vocal crowds – the company had every reason to feel that it might be their subtlety of approach that prevented Deacon Blue's records coming across to people on the radio in the way that they might.

Thus it was that in December of 1987, the band rerecorded

'Dignity' with American producer Bob Clearmountain at the helm. Clearmountain was no stranger to the band's musical style, having spruced up Bruce Springsteen's prospective singles for radio play, given them extra definition and smoother lines ideal for radio formatting. At other stages, he had helped revive Bryan Ferry's career, helped make the Rolling Stones more radio-friendly and despatched Simple Minds into the stadium bracket with his clinical production and sharp understanding of just what would sound good on the radio. His ability to mix instruments so they charged rather than dripped from a car radio made the difference between a hit record and an also-ran.

Clearmountain was widely regarded within the industry as the AOR rock producer *par excellence* and as such, his time was very valuable. Nevertheless, CBS were willing to make the investment and the master tape that this alliance produced indicated just how wise a decision that had been. Released into the fairly slow post-Christmas market of January 1988, 'Dignity' finally reached the charts, peaking at No. 31. This was by no means a hit, but it gave Deacon Blue the foothold that they required. Having reached the charts once, they were guaranteed airplay for the next single, then the next and so on. CBS had finally got the Deacon Blue bandwagon rolling and from there on in, it would prove to be unstoppable.

Here was the point at which opinions began to diverge – those members of the press that had taken the introspection of *Raintown* to their hearts were affronted by Clearmountain's brazen reworking of a good song, stealing it away from its soulful roots and placing it in the rock marketplace. Those who hated Deacon Blue from the off for their stadium potential saw this rerecording as yet another cynical marketing ploy and proof positive that here was a group more interested in making money than making music. Pretty quickly, Deacon Blue were running short of friends in influential places.

As ever, if you step back from the emotion of the time, it's easy to see that their supporters were being too precious about the music. By making a few changes to one song, the group were introducing more people to their debut LP, thereby ensuring that a second would be produced in the fullness of time. For this, those detractors should have been grateful for if the band had continued to fail commercially, there were no guarantees that there would have been another Deacon Blue album. However, fandom does not always operate within the strict confines of logic and so these early fanatics were also disappointed to see their pet group being discovered by more and more people, destroying their exclusivity.

For Deacon Blue and Ross in particular, the opportunity to work with Clearmountain must have been a godsend, as close to an open goal as the notoriously fickle music business is likely to offer. As a token of confidence from CBS it must have been refreshing and a source of relief and it was not a chance they were going to miss. For those who did not like the new version, they had the option to go back to *Raintown* and play that version of the song. From Ross' point of view, this was simply a new setting for his work – his innate curiosity would have drawn him to working with Clearmountain anyway, even had it turned into a fiasco. For him, his artistic credentials were not on the line as a result of this collaboration.

Ross was nobody's fool. He admitted to *Sounds*, 'We must be losing about £200 a day at the moment. But we've got good sponsors and they obviously feel we're a good investment.' He knew that, no matter what your artistic ideals might be, if you wanted to communicate with a large audience you had to accept economic realities.

CBS had very good economic reasons for pushing Deacon Blue into the limelight, of course, since a lot of hopes were riding on the band. Their executives would have gone along with the standard music industry projection that by the early nineties, rock would have fragmented in sales terms with most albums selling on compact disc to an older audience. Deacon Blue had been signed up because of their obvious appeal to a more mature audience and the time had come for CBS to protect themselves by doing whatever was necessary to deliver them a hit record.

To be fair to CBS and the likes of Muff Winwood, there was a genuine belief that Deacon Blue had something to offer and had the ability to become a major act. Musically they were clearly excellent, Ross and McIntosh were a formidable vocal duo. All that was left was to bring them to public attention so that less and less promotion would be required to sell what were clearly very good songs that people would want.

If only life were that straightforward. Deacon Blue had by now alienated a very large percentage of their media friends who were distressed to see them playing the pop game in what they felt was such a blatant manner. Matters were considerably worsened in August 1988 when *Raintown*, now eighteen months old and already carefully ensconced within the record collection of every real fan of the group, was repackaged along with a free album called *Riches*, which was essentially a collection of the band's deleted B-sides. Quite rightly, the press took this to be a case of urine extraction gone mad – were CBS determined to squeeze Deacon Blue's supporters until the pips squeaked just to try and get a few more sales from an old record?

As a collection of songs, *Riches* was admirable. The quality of the material was solid if unspectacular, though the piano version of 'Raintown' actually eclipsed the original album version. The take on Van Morrison's 'Angeliou' was invigorating and enlightening and a number of the other tracks might easily have found their way onto the debut album. All that was swept away by a tide of anger within press circles – and among many fans too, it must be said. They were indignant that to get hold of this collection, limited to just 20,000 copies, fans were required to buy the album again. This was an appalling piece of exploitation on the part of CBS and Deacon Blue came out of it with no credit whatsoever; *Riches* should have been quietly put out as a mid-price album for fans to pick up at their leisure, rather than being forced to immediately shell out for the same *Raintown* album before the 20,000 copies sold out.

This crass piece of commercialization did the trick though, for *Raintown* hit No. 14 in the charts and on the back of the attendant publicity went on to sell in excess of 350,000 copies and stay in the top fifty for a further year. It was possibly this success, coupled with the improved but still disappointing performance of 'When Will You (Make My Telephone Ring)' and 'Chocolate Girl' in the singles chart, that finally convinced CBS that they had an album act on their hands for whom singles would be little more than a diversion.

As the press grew colder, the commercial flames burned brighter and the band were able to sell out sizeable venues the length and breadth of the land to very enthusiastic crowds. CBS' decision was thoroughly vindicated in commercial terms though they could count themselves inordinately lucky at the forbearance of Deacon Blue's supporters. A less fanatical fan base might by now have told CBS where to get off with their marketing gimmicks, but as Tom Morton had noted in a live review, Deacon Blue were very definitely 'a fan's band' and for very good reasons, for despite Ross' protests, they were a group in whom you could put your trust for they did not disappoint. If this was your kind of music, you could be certain that Deacon Blue would perform it well and in entertaining fashion. And if you wanted to delve a little deeper and take something more from them than just a good night out, you were welcome to do that too. The press like to kid themselves that they represent real music fans, a *cognoscenti* for whom music is all; and fashionable, 'happening' music at that. But in reality, the bulk of the nation's music is bought by people who scarcely ever pick up a copy of the music papers, people unconcerned by the latest musical trends but who know what they like. You might argue that the musical health of the nation would be improved if more people were interested in the views of *Melody Maker*, you might even be right, but that isn't the way it is. With the current status quo, Deacon Blue and their ilk are unlikely to be troubled by the *New Musical Express*' attitude to them.

Ironically, fans wanted Deacon Blue to be all things to all

people. They were undeniably moved by the songs on *Raintown* and the private nature of some of that music, but at the same time they wanted a good time rock 'n' roll show and reassurance that there was always something to hope for or to aspire to whenever they ventured out to see their concerts. Ross was happy enough to be the provider of the proverbial big night out. 'For me, a good night out is something that lasts into the next week and beyond. A good night out can be a brilliant feeling when something really gets to you. It can be a record, a gig, an experience or a chance meeting with someone. It's something that can actually change you in some way. Sometimes you can see a band play live and if it's a good night, you still get the buzz from it a few days later.'

This of course remained central to Ross' philosophy, that music could change people, might cleanse them or change their view of things. It's sad then that once they became estranged, the press were eager to think of him and the band as providing an easy fix of conscience-salving angst for concerned audiences who agreed with Ross' lectures from the rock pulpit, then went home to worry about fiddling their tax returns. This was of course typical of the music press' snobbery where anything that sells is automatically awful unless, like REM or U2, they get a note of dispensation from the editor.

Nevertheless, Deacon Blue's new-found popularity, founded on what many judges felt to be a clearly inferior version of 'Dignity', did beg the question. Why were they now so popular? Were people suddenly taking some notice of Ross' blue-collar perspective? Were they catching on to his lyrical swipes at the state of the country? Were they there to swoon along to his melancholic love songs? Questions like these are fraught with difficulties – answer them successfully and you have a place in the top ten for life.

For the time being, though, Deacon Blue remained on the live treadmill, basking in and capitalizing on their new-found prominence. After a while, the great adventure began to pale a little, Dougie Vipond worrying that, 'These days you don't get the chance to talk to each other. You sleep in the van or you sit in your room but then, when you get on stage, it all clicks.' Ross sympathized with Vipond's worries but reflected, 'A year ago we would have jumped at the chance to play all the gigs we complain about having to do now.'

Perhaps Deacon Blue's greatest problem was their naive honesty in press interviews, quotes coming back to haunt them in subsequent years. It was very easy indeed to portray them as gold-diggers, only in it for the money, when Lorraine McIntosh went on record as saying, 'Failure? If you're in a band there's no way you can even consider the prospect. I wouldn't say that we never look beyond tomorrow, but we'd never dare to plan or think beyond the next studio session or the next tour.' This could come across as arrogance, but it was really just an expression of the armour plating that has to protect a group's collective ego in times of crisis. It's common to all groups who hope to go on to greater things – without it none of them would have got out of a rehearsal room. Her qualification set the record straight as to her real motives – 'I wouldn't want to be doing anything else' – but this was the kind of addendum that gets lost in the cuttings file. The promotion of a little more mystique might not have done Deacon Blue a disservice.

That they were becoming a little bewildered by their new success and surroundings was borne out by another interview that Lorraine McIntosh gave to *Melody Maker*. On the subject of money, she told them, 'I've become really sick [of it]. When we started going to Holland and Germany doing TV shows, they put you in places like the Munich Hilton. I remember sitting in this room one night and it was the size of my friends' houses and it would cost them three weeks' Giros to stay the night. You begin to think this is preposterous. I don't want a flat with a nice cheese plant in the window and nice books on shelves that I'll never read. I want a flat with ordinary patterned wallpaper to bring me back down to earth.'

Reflecting on home, it was clear that the incessant touring hadn't changed the compassionate heart that was at the centre of the group's work. 'Home isn't really Scotland, it's Glasgow . . . when we go abroad, we hear people saying, "Oh, we hear Glasgow's changed now," or that it's a new city and that makes me a bit sick. Although the city centre's been tarted up . . . when you drive to the outskirts you pass these sprawling housing estates with 50,000 people, no pubs, no shops, nothing to do . . . it's as sad as that. They stick 50,000 people in an area and give them nothing.'

For an indignant media, this straightforward openness was now a reason to attack Deacon Blue. Their songs weren't sufficiently oblique, musically they were too linear, appealing to the lowest common denominator, and so on. Yet they were still hawking round the *Raintown* album that had been so well received. Finally though, in May 1988, the *Raintown* circus ground to a halt as the group prepared to record the all important follow-up. Now the spotlight was very much on them as a group from whom great things were expected.

CHAPTER EIGHT

Few bands could have worked harder than Deacon Blue in the seventeen months from January 1987 through to May 1988 when they got down to the business of recording again. It's a well-worn cliché but it's true to say that the group had ridden a roller coaster through that period. They'd crafted a record they were very happy with, found that its less obvious charms were not readily translating themselves to a wider audience, saw the singles fail too, yet were more than capable of throwing themselves into their exhausting concert timetable, a whole-hearted commitment which was to pay dividends later.

Finding their own audience was a long-drawn-out business but one which was ultimately rewarding. Sadly, in terms of the future perception of the band, the sterling work that they put in was ignored. Deacon Blue really did succeed in creating a true bond of affection, a sense of community between band and audience, people responding to their unaffected simplicity of approach, their commitment and their obvious unrestrained joy at being able to play their songs live. However, the casual observer, prompted by sniping press comments, remembered Deacon Blue as that group that were hyped to success with rerecordings, gimmicky marketing ploys, and bonus albums. It all suggested a manufactured group that would prove to have no real substance in the long run.

The band must have been aware of this development, even though they still won the occasional bit of praise, *New Musical Express* calling 'When Will You (Make My Telephone Ring)' when it was rereleased 'one of the most intelligent songs of the week . . . more traces of soul here than on your average pop platter'. Even so, Ross must have been worried that their new audience, devoted though it was, might eventually be fragmented both by the criticism and by any more heavy-handed pieces of marketing courtesy of CBS. Fans might forgive the *Raintown* and *Riches* debacle, but if CBS felt the need to take similar action in the future, they might not take so kindly to further exploitation.

For their second album, *When the World Knows Your Name*, Deacon Blue quite clearly took a very different approach to writing and recording. Ross made no bones about the change in style. 'The time is right to bring people into what we're doing. If Lloyd Cole hadn't called his album *Mainstream* two years ago, that's what I would've called this one. Maybe we should've called it *Showbiz*!'

Talking to *Hot Press*, Ross went further. 'Basically, we wanted to challenge what we'd done very strongly. With the new record we were aiming to make more of a Deacon Blue record, which reflected the fact that we've been together as a group for almost three years, which was more representative of us live, and which brought out the individual contributions to the overall sound. The producer on *Raintown*, Jon Kelly, wasn't really into taking lots of time working on individual sounds but was more interested in keeping the vibe going and bringing out something in the band that was almost spiritual. And that worked, it was the ideal thing to do for a first record. The success of [*When the World Knows Your Name*] is that, although it's taken longer to put together in the studio, it sounds more like the band live.'

The most interesting question is just how did this change come about? Certainly *Raintown* had been a slow starter but it had come through more than successfully in the end, being a favourite record with many, many people. From that standpoint, it might have been obvious, attractive even, to do *Raintown 2 – the Thunderstorm*, but this was never on Ross' agenda. He'd already made it clear back in 1987 that *Raintown* would be their only record in that style, though the reasons were numerous. 'We could easily have gone back in the studio with Jon producing and got the same vibe going,' Ross agreed. 'But it would have effectively put us back two years. My friends have pointed out that with this new album, there's no "Dignity", "Chocolate Girl" or "Spencer Tracy", which were the three landmark songs on the first one, and that's quite deliberate. We wanted to show that we could move forward. You can't stand still, you can't get caught up in your own trousers and do a Blue Nile where you spend ages so self-obsessed that you get nothing done.'

One of the goals that Ross had set himself was to maintain his self-respect and honesty as a performer. 'I think it's important to strive for honesty in songwriting. When I was younger, I wouldn't have thought that, but now I think it is important to write about things that I actually believe in. If there is an element of bluff in a song, the audience are going to be the first people to pick up on it. You can't expect people to take you seriously unless you are facing up to your own situation.'

Lorraine McIntosh backed up the shift in emphasis that would be necessary on *When the World Knows Your Name*, explaing that, 'We haven't really been in Glasgow that much this past year, so it would be false to try and keep up the pretence that we're all broke and that we never get out of the city. If anything, we're never there. We travel a lot and we're not particularly broke, so it would be false to hold on to some image of Ricky sitting in a back room with no money and the rain pouring down. There's no way we could do another set of songs about being unemployed and trapped when we're not.'

Ross and Deacon Blue had moved on from those years of

struggle in Glasgow. If they weren't yet at the summit of the pop industry, they'd certainly set out from base camp, ready for the inevitable conquest. Dealing in the language of the defeated or the misunderstood would only be regarded as self-serving and hypocritical. Whether he liked it or not, Ross now felt compelled to turn his attention to another side of life, another version of its drama, without dwelling unduly on its down side.

In fairness, as a genuinely creative artist, Ross, having found his feet on that first record, quite naturally wanted to test his abilities rather than hone a style in which he had already proved his talent to his own satisfaction. This refusal to simply retrace his steps for security's sake was, on the face of it, wholly admirable. However, by suggesting that he was involved in compiling a record that was out to take the mainstream market by the scruff of the neck, he wasn't accumulating too many brownie points.

The admission that success is a goal, that you are out to capture a wide audience, is not one that people in this country take too kindly. Whereas in America, every encouragement is given to the wide-eyed youngster who wants it all and wants it now – that's the American dream, after all – Britons are supposed to be rather more reticent; it's supposedly preferable to struggle in a garret, showing your work to a few people than broadcasting to millions.

It's a charge that was levelled against U2, against the Police and against countless others – that to reach the masses you have to shave off all your little idiosyncrasies, all the things that might make you unusual and difficult to market, consequently neutering all the things that made you interesting in the first place. The mass market does not deal in those qualities, but in easy listening, music that doesn't require commitment or emotion. The argument has some truth but conveniently ignores such exceptions as the Beatles and REM.

To berate Deacon Blue for being successful is as sensible as chastising a sheepdog for rounding up sheep – success was what Deacon Blue were built for, and that is not meant in any pejorative way. Deacon Blue were designed to play big music on a big stage. Yet nothing is that simple. They embody a great rock 'n' roll contradiction – small-town dreams played out on the massive stage. Ross accepted this paradox early on in discussions about *Raintown*.

'A lot of people listen to records alone and build up a relationship with certain songs,' he remarked. 'It's like a friend they pull out at certain times when they need it. Records have always been very personal things to me. To some people, music is a very communal thing. I've never been able to see that. This is very private music. It's also rock music, unashamedly and absolutely. We don't come from any other tradition. I like rock's clever use of clichés. I like it when you listen to someone like Ry Cooder where you can't even begin to think where the originality comes in but the magic is definitely there. My ambition is to narrow all my songs down to one room. I've got it down to one town and it doesn't seem to want to budge any further.'

Yet implicit in that consideration of his own muse was the acceptance that, coming from the rock tradition, the music had to go on to the stages of the world, for without touring, the band could not grow commercially and would therefore miss its opportunity to make more records. These were conflicts that Ross wrestled with in contemplating the direction for the second record, a record which he knew must reach more people. They grasped this inherent need, by returning to a simpler instrumentation for the record, making the translation to live performance much easier. 'I've always liked these basic, rootsy instruments so for me it's great. It's funny but if you do something with synthesizers and top of the range technology it can date quite easily.'

It's been noted that Ross was wary of allowing CBS any further licence with 'unusual' marketing schemes, but he also recognized that Deacon Blue were the kind of group who were being groomed as a long-term act and had to sell large quantities of albums. This had its inevitable musical consequences which will be addressed later, but other factors were combining to alter the Deacon Blue musical landscape too. The band maintained their hectic pace right up until May when work began on the second album. Reviews of those last shows were particularly interesting, especially since by now, the heavyweight newspapers were on their tail. Writing for the *Guardian* in April, Bob Flynn noted, 'It's hard to deny the band's march from small-time brooding to massive attack. *Raintown* was a vital attempt at Scottish soul and [the crowd] ached for and with them as Ross' voice went from smooth to rough during the long set. Special mention here to the powerful vocals of Lorraine McIntosh who sounds as if she has come out of Detroit rather than Glasgow – a description which could apply indeed to the whole band . . . Deacon Blue are deliberately dramatic – Ross has been accused of false anguish but he means it and does not hestitate to show his feelings through his songs and between-song chat . . . escape and dignity in the face of a sinking reality.'

While Scottish critics still warmed to the group, perhaps possessing a greater intuitive feel for the dreams exposed in *Raintown*, they were still ready to note that the group were developing a harder edge, that 'massive attack' usurping some of the soulful swing employed on record. *Melody Maker*'s Penny Kiley, on the other hand, suggested that, 'For half a set, this feels like background music. Tasteful, clean, pleasant, straight-forward . . . "Loaded" finally transcends detachment as powerful repetition turns a song into eighties blues and another repetition turns band and audience into one and "community" becomes more than the usual community singing. There is joy in the audience and Deacon Blue have, finally, touched something.'

Kiley also touched on the 'rather tedious earnestness of [1987's] student union gigs', belief being the antithesis of the studied cool that the press demands. It was those student shows that triggered something of a transformation in Deacon Blue. To get people's attention, Ross chose to shout rather than whisper, a thoroughly understandable reaction. That necessarily led to the loss of their songs' understatement and its replacement with something rather closer to a rabble-rousing approach which engaged audiences out for a raucous evening but which often did little to improve the music itself.

Naturally tiring of the student union rounds, happy to have moved into the more comfortable surroundings of larger venues, Ross and the band were looking to maintain that rate of progress, hence proclamations about the mainstream. Musically, they were tighter, harder than ever before and it was inevitable that, for better or worse, this would spill over into the new record.

It appeared that Deacon Blue were about to fall foul of what was quickly to become the U2 syndrome as the post *Rattle and Hum* backlash began, U2 being accused of broadening their appeal via huge, but ultimately empty gestures and in being more concerned with success than the music. From his vantage point, Ross took issue. 'I think the press have a problem with bands like Deacon Blue because we're successful as well. They'll like what we're doing when we're not successful . . . when people sell records, their music doesn't just go to the wall. I take great issue with [the press] about U2 [and *Rattle and Hum*]. I loved it. [*Melody Maker*] said "gospel music is crap". I mean, who is writing this? I couldn't believe it. It's the most uplifting music there is and a great record. ["I Still Haven't Found What I'm Looking For"], I absolutely loved it. And I love the record, what they're doing. I can understand why people slate successful bands. But I think it's very immature. I think it's a security thing. People don't like to be seen liking something which is safe. They'd much rather be cool and trendy.'

Another influence that hardened the musical landscape came in the shape of that 'doctrinal upfulness' of which a reviewer had spoken. With their ambitious aggression, sometimes confused with arrogance, Deacon Blue were always, inevitably, having to go in search of the next level of achievement. Failure to move on would undermine their central philosophy of optimistic perseverance, letting down thousands who had come to believe in their 'message' such as it was. Relentless ambition tends to lead to a hardening of the musical arteries, power driven bluster replacing the tender virtues that had initially characterized the group.

It was a trap of which they were aware, yet they seemed powerless to avoid it. On the original release of 'Dignity', Ross had looked ahead to the long concert tours that lay before them. 'I know that most pop groups like the idea of seduction. They set out to seduce their audiences. Seduction is a dodgy word, isn't it? It has notions of owning people, charming people over to your side. I don't like the idea of people throwing themselves over to our music. Abandonment is a great idea but it worries me because it's all so power-orientated. Sexual language, seduction, the art of chatting-up, ownership and power seem to be a part of the same idea. I don't want much to do with that. I don't particularly care about Deacon Blue being a sexual rock group. It's not that I associate sex with power but the actual language seems so bound up with it. If anything, the words have to be brought back into the language in a fresh, new way.'

Ross, however, seemed uncertain of how to engineer this feat and, in dispensing with seduction as a tool, Deacon Blue instead seemed determined to go honestly onto the offensive, bludgeoning people into submission with that 'massive attack'. Demos of the new album illustrated that traces of that live power were filtering their way into the songs, but pieces such as 'Sad Loved Girl' and 'Long Window to Love' did not seem to be too far removed temperamentally from *Raintown*, demonstrating that Ross had lost none of his ear for a classic hook or beautiful melody.

Whatever the rationale behind it, Ross was clear that the new record would be different. His most obvious problem was to harness the band's new confidence to songs that were not ruined by any excess – that Deacon Blue trod a tightrope between power and bluster from their earliest incarnations, not always with the greatest of success, has been demonstrated. But Deacon Blue had now had the opportunity of growing together through a couple of exciting years. Such was the internal dynamic of the band, this second album would feature far more input from the musicians, even though Ross was clearly the captain of the ship.

There was little time for reflection given the hectic pace that they were setting, but Ross was keen to assert the virtues of the group and of what they were doing. 'I saw Lone Justice at the Marquee recently and there was this girl [Maria McKee] who just wanted to overpower everybody, she just wanted to go totally further than was necessary. Then I saw Alison Moyet and she was doing it all wrong and I just felt like saying, "Oh no no no!" People don't want to go home after a gig and have a curry. They want to cry or fall in love. It's more important than all those other things.'

With such powerful motivations, it's hard to see how Ross could fail to follow his artistic instincts. And yet the feeling persists that *When the World Knows Your Name*, for all its massive success, was not the record it could and should have been. *Raintown* had been created in blissful isolation. *When the World Knows Your Name* was concocted in a pressure cooker. Lorraine McIntosh conceded the point, submitting that, 'I think this album will be a lot harder to do than the first one, where there was no previous work for it to be judged against, but it's going to be much better. It will still be really melodic, but harder-sounding.'

The weight of expectations certainly altered the atmosphere in the Deacon Blue camp, with each member of the sextet making strenuous efforts to ensure that no one in their burgeoning fan club could possibly be disappointed. As can so often be the case, that effort is often the ingredient that sends things awry. By trying too hard to catch the magic, the inspiration that made a demo sound so good is lost in the sterile, squeaky-clean finished product.

Certainly the demos sounded fine. The sound was broader, it's true, but there was no chest-beating or proclamations of 'Hear me!' Yet by the time they got on to the album, the music was polished, sparkling, manufactured and generally soulless, the gravest slur that could be applied to Deacon Blue, devotees of the soul mood as they were. Ross had already set out to achieve its clinical lines prior to recording, however. 'Death and glory, I suppose,' was how he looked forward to it. 'I'd like it to be a very happy, sparkling album . . . I think it will be quite hard to get this one together and maybe [there] won't even be another one. But that doesn't really matter. I think it's good when something is done and stopped – it's really healthy. Things that go on too long become the most annoying.'

That Ross was sincere with these threats became clear when he did finally call a close to Deacon Blue in 1994, but clearly *When the World Knows Your Name* was not the record to end with for it was not the summation of Deacon Blue's work. Nevertheless, Ross did betray a suggestion that perhaps his musical outlook was being changed by his attachment to a major record company. 'As long as we make records, I'm happy. The only reason I'm glad [the singles] are in the top forty is basically because CBS will give us the grant to make another album. That's what it all boils down to. There's no other reason for them to do it than that. "We really believe in you guys . . . we are the family of music," and all that.'

Obviously Ross' relationship with CBS was no longer the 'all friends together' one it had been the previous year. It was clear that Ross was rapidly losing patience with the manœuvrings of the industry. But the scent of compromise was very much in the air with statements such as these, all the more so when Ross added, a little unconvincingly, 'When you make any record you want it to have a broad appeal, but without compromising the unique things that you do. You don't deliberately water it down. People generally set out to make good records. Also, if you're like Deacon Blue and you're on a swing, suddenly what the record company people are thinking is singles . . . and we woke up to the fact that we had songs that were singles. We've got seven, or maybe even eight on this album and we're probably going to release six just so it keeps the record on the radio. We want to sell lots of records and I don't think there's anything wrong with admitting that.'

From a personal standpoint, Ross was caught between two stools – though he was keen to sell records, at the same time he did not welcome the intrusion into his life that pop stardom would inevitably bring in its wake. 'Someone said to me, "You can always make records which are full of love songs." The one thing I've always wanted to do is be a songwriter. Not necessarily a performer. I could easily be commissioned to just go off and write songs, y'know. The only thing is, they'd have to be love songs. If I had to spend the rest of my life sitting in a room doing it, that'd be fine. It wouldn't be a problem. There's so much scope . . . All this business, it's not about being famous. It's about a few years' worth of good work. If you can produce one great album in your career, you've probably done fifty per cent better than a lot of bands. If you produce a couple that's great . . . I *much* prefer [anonymity] . . . certain bits are nice. It's nice when someone comes up and says they like my music. As a songwriter you never get that. But compared to the hassles, songwriting is . . . well, you can't make a living from it basically.'

There were already suggestions that the relationship between Deacon Blue and CBS was starting to deteriorate as the company went in search of hits, hits, hits. The band were able to meet these expectations but it was clear that a rift was starting to develop. It might conceivably have crossed his mind that by delivering the goods to CBS this time around, elevating Deacon Blue to the big league, he would be buying himself freedom in the future to do whatever he would like to do. Equally possible is that he was genuinely intrigued by the challenge of breaking into a completely different market; after all, as a songwriter you want your songs to be heard. The level of compromise you make to achieve that goal is up to you.

Opinion is thoroughly split on just what did motivate Deacon Blue to produce such an upfront album as *When the World Knows Your Name*, whether it was an organic creation that drew on their experiences or simply a hit-laden platter to satisfy company demands. But it was no real surprise then that Bob Clearmountain was employed to remix the bulk of the album before it hit the shops.

'It's almost as if when you do anything that's vaguely within the mainstream, make the kind of record that's inevitably going to end up in the HMV top sixty rack for a few months, be it a hard rock record, a dance record or a folk record, you get that thrown at you, "Aha, you're going for the American market!" And the fact of the matter is that you are! And you're going for Europe, Australia and everywhere else.'

Ross made a noose for his own neck: the desire to crack America was the aim that dare not speak its name. It was more revealing, though, of his own insecurity than the ambition of the group. The impression was given that Ross had had his struggles over the years, had seen Woza disintegrate when success seemed likely and had undergone a tense period when it looked as though Deacon Blue might not reach their audience. Now, from a position of strength, it was a perfectly acceptable human reaction to set your jaw against ever slipping back into that miserable uncertainty. Ross wrote songs, good ones, just as he had in 1984. Now that he was a prominent figure in British music, he meant to exploit that position to the full before anyone could take it away from him, cementing himself into a role he could grow into. Ross took the logical route and provided CBS with an album brimming with hit singles which, given the Clearmountain treatment, could not fail.

If Deacon Blue are not to be allowed entrance to the Elysian musical fields wherein romp the Beatles, the Stones, Van Morrison, Jimi Hendrix, U2, Talking Heads and those others who have brought about a fundamental shift in the musical axis, might it not be reasonable to suggest that they did provide a great service to the world of popular music in bringing down the curtain on the coy political games fought out between pundits, performers and accountants? In their desire to achieve as much as they possibly could, musically and materially, there was nothing unusual about them. Where they diverged from the norm was in not pretending to be only in it for spiritual reasons.

John Lennon eventually came clean about the motivations that pushed him and the Beatles into the stratosphere, recalling that he and Paul McCartney would often settle down in a hotel room while on tour and deliberately 'write a swimming pool', a new chart-topper that would pay for some addition to their respective households. A few other rockers in the interim have sheepishly agreed that success has motivated them but few have held ambition to be such a virtue as Deacon Blue did in 1988/9.

In such behaviour, were Deacon Blue signifying the end of innocence and unrealistic expectations of record company benevolence? You have only to scan through the lists of groups who made one album, watched it fail and then scurried back into the obscurity from which they came to grasp the fact that record companies have never been run on charitable grounds; Apple Corps in the late sixties is the most notable exception and that succeeded in breaking up the Beatles, so there seems no good reason why a record company should model its principles on Oxfam.

Record companies have always been voracious beasts out to look after their shareholders. Since they reap their rewards from the propagation of 'art' they could rarely come clean about this but by the end of the Thatcherite eighties, denying it was counter-productive. In order to seek further investment, they had to be bold and thrusting, financially rapacious with a clear eye for the bottom line. By this time, the music industry was no longer an island but a sector of the multi-national conglomerate-based entertainment industry worth multi-millions of dollars per year. As the final straw, by the late eighties, the record companies had perpetrated one of the greatest marketing scams of the century – the compact disc. Why buy your entire record collection once when you can buy it twice? It was clear to the least concerned observer that the record industry was after the big bucks and that it generally got what it wanted. Any kind of pretence was futile.

Ricky Ross and Deacon Blue were big enough to meet that challenge head on, without obfuscation. Their response was unequivocal: The record company wants healthy sales. We want to continue making records. It may be an exaggeration, but Deacon Blue might have set up the most honest relationship in existence between a group and its audience and that is to be applauded, whatever your view of the music and the motive itself.

The other debate which they set into motion is an age-old one. What exactly is wrong in selling lots of records to a mass of people? Does it automatically mean selling out? For many, the fiercest defenders of 'art' as a concept, it is a betrayal, a dilution of all the strongest flavours into a lightly-sparkling cordial suitable for the less discerning palate. This is an attitude tainted with snobbery for if a million people buy an album, lodging it securely at the top of the charts for weeks on end, who is to say that they are wrong?

Ross accepted this factor within music, turning the accusation in on himself when discussing *When the World Knows Your Name*. 'With *The Joshua Tree*, it's just so consistent from beginning to end. I was talking with friends the other night about our new record and they were finding with successive listens that things were coming out and I thought back to the U2 record and the first single that was released, "With or Without You", and I think there's a tendency to dismiss singles at first whereas now that's without doubt my favourite track. In many ways I feel the same way about "Real Gone Kid", that because it's been out and played so much, people will just dismiss it. You've got to leave it for six months and then come back. I'm still very proud of that song but I'm sure people will put the record on and go, "Oh, heard that before, let's go on to something else." I'd have to say that one of the most successful songs for me in terms of writing and the band performing is "Wages Day", because it's so simple . . . but because of the commercial thing, because it's a single, people disregard it.'

We hear plenty of voices clamouring for democracy, yet the

album charts are the voice of musical democracy, a weekly general election to discover what is popular. Now democracy may not always produce the result that you're looking for, even four times running, but it is a snapshot of what people want. A lot of people want Deacon Blue records. Very few people want Cranes records at present, but those that do live with them for months on end. Which is better?

The point is that neither is inherently better or worse. Every time Michael Bolton appears on the radio, the return of capital punishment may suddenly seem like a good idea, but the fact is that he is very popular and so those people who wish to buy his records should have the opportunity to do so without being the object of media derision. It was a theme to which Ross quickly warmed, although opponents might legitimately claim that he would, wouldn't he? 'I was reading in the *New Musical Express* about Matt Johnson [The The], about how he thinks his music's more important than others – I think that's fucking shite! I've never read so much claptrap in my life. If you believe in pop music, you believe in the plurality of pop music, that yours is as good as anyone else's – that's the whole basis. It's popular music, it's not the arts, it's not some kind of pyramid. It's pop music, it's no more than that.'

Nevertheless, Ross was sufficiently concerned with wider opinions to admit to some regrets over the way in which the music business operates. 'The problem with the record industry is we've got this cut-throat approach – there are some albums that [are talked about] but as far as a lot of the folk who go into record shops, they'll never get round to buying them because they've got five quid in their pocket – they've got a choice between a Deacon Blue album [and something else].' The music business is, by definition, a competition, but Ross was simply mature enough to accept that fact. More interestingly, would he be able to retain his ideals intact in the face of the corporate onslaught?

Above: Lorraine McIntosh and Ricky Ross, July 1990. (Mick Hutson/Redferns)

Right: Godson of soul: Ricky Ross wearing his inspiration, July 1990. (Mick Hutson/Redferns)

Above: Fellow Hoodlums: Ricky Ross and Ewen Vernal, 1991. (Mick Hutson/Redferns)

Below: Girl (and boys) on film: Lorraine McIntosh, James Prine and Ricky Ross in The Big Picture, 1991. (Mick Hutson/Redferns)

Opposite page: Ricky Ross, 1991. (Mick Hutson/Redferns)

Above: Signing on, April 1993: Ewen Vernal, Dougie Vipond, Graeme Kelling, Lorraine McIntosh, Ricky Ross, James Prine. (Susan Moore/Redferns)

Left: 'Waddya mean, it's in the sale already?' Ricky Ross hunts for bargains, April 1993. (Susan Moore/Redferns)

Right: Post-modernism ahoy. Ricky Ross, Hammersmith Apollo, 21 April 1993. (Steve Gillett/Redferns)

Below: 'I'm saying nothing.' Ricky Ross, 1993. (Susan Moore/Redferns)

Left: Ewen Vernal, 1993. (Steve Gillett/Redferns)

Below: Lorraine McIntosh. (N. Kitson/Redferns)

Opposite page: A loaded Ricky Ross at the Greenbelt Festival. (Steve Gillett/Redferns)

Right: Graeme Kelling, 1993. (Susan Moore/Redferns)

Below: Coal not dole: Deacon Blue provide a failed Bono look-alike with job training, 1993. (Susan Moore/Redferns)

CHAPTER NINE

Second albums have often been termed 'difficult' throughout rock history. The cliché is you have a lifetime to write your first album and six months to write the second, if you get the chance to make one. Ricky Ross was, fortunately, a pretty prolific songwriter and so there was no shortage of material queuing up for a slot on the finished record. A shortage of material would not be an excuse the band could fall back on in the event of unfavourable sales or reviews.

Naturally enough, since so much had happened to the band in such a short space of time, it was inevitable that rather than being an exercise in introspection as *Raintown* had been, *When the World Knows Your Name* would be a little more reactive, a response to the situations they had been in and what they had seen of the world. When a record is trying to be outgoing in such a way, the obvious thing to do is to turn up the musical heat a little to reach people, rather than trying to gently draw them in to a very private world.

The songs were reactive too, in part to the pigeonholing that had gone on. There were two distinct strains of critical opinion on Deacon Blue. The first, which has been thoroughly explored, was that live performance was changing the character of the group into some quasi-metallic outfit. Other opinion took *Raintown* at surface value and treated them as morose commentators on a decaying town, peddling soft rock torch songs. Both had a germ of truth but neither provided the complete picture of a band far more complex than many would credit.

Ross was as engagingly open about the change in the band as one had come to expect him to be. 'I think *When the World Knows Your Name* is actually a *Deacon Blue* record, where the other one was a record by a group that had been together for six months. I had a complete shock [in mid-88] when I realized, being interviewed by someone, that they had no idea that we thought of ourselves as a rock band. Then I'd read these press things where we were compared to Prefab Sprout – but wait a minute, this is not where we want to be at all – no disrespect to them.'

Not only did Ross feel that Deacon Blue were being misrepresented in that regard, leading them to flex their musical muscularity a little in response, but the enormous, slow-burning success of *Raintown* meant that he felt trapped by a record that was in the past as far as he was concerned. Anyone that had had Deacon Blue recommended to them would only have *Raintown* as a point of reference whereas the group itself had clearly progressed beyond that stage.

Ross elaborated further, suggesting that comparisons between that album and their new platter were invidious. '*Raintown* did box office, but not exactly overnight. It's the kind of album you find you're still listening to when other, more short-term effective chocolate boxes are relegated to the back of your archive . . . if there'd been a *Raintown* songsheet passed around at cub scout camp, I'd want to get hold of that, rip it up and start again. *Raintown* became a kind of embarrassment, in the sense that it hung around – you wanted to kick it out and say, "Go home, fuck off, have your breakfast, do something else." We really wanted to move on, but it was still there, people were still listening to it two years after we made it. Whether this one will manage to do that . . .'

Whether *When the World Knows Your Name* was designed as the short-term chocolate box to obviate that problem in the future is unclear. Certainly a lot of thought and a lot of hard work went into it, including the selection of the title. It was deliberately tongue-in-cheek, not a characteristic for which Deacon Blue and Ricky Ross had been most noted in the past, another example of their desire to start again in some capacity. The truth was, of course, that while they had become one of the biggest bands in Britain, beyond this septic isle they had barely made an impression and were still trekking around the club circuit, a useful down to earth exercise for them.

'I had no doubts when we chose the title the fun that would be had with it. It was like leaving the door open for cynics – "Yeah! Here we go! Bon Jovi!" I thought it was a good idea, it would sort out the sheep from the goats really. People coming up to us and going, "Love the title of the album – so true isn't it?"' By the same token, there was a little truth in the title, for Deacon Blue, especially Ross and McIntosh, were now celebrities. The concentration on them wasn't always wholly welcome either, and the album title acted as a wry dig at that and at the workload they'd endured to reach their particular position in the pop field.

Ross did maintain that the new record was not one about their new-found fame, though Andrew Collins of *New Musical Express* suggested that it 'reads like an autobiography, a report from the frontline of fame, if you like. The lyrics are honed down and steeped in starry-eyed self-reference.' Ross was forced to concur with that assessment in part, explaining, 'There is a wider title, but I think it's more like the angle from which things are looked at. If you're not stuck in a place constantly for six months, then clearly you're not going to write as intensely about that place and those streets – but what you are going to do is, every time you come back to the place, it's gonna hit you again each time. Which is what happens to us.'

Going further into the record's genesis, Ross noted that, 'Most of the success has happened [since August 1988] and most of the album was planned out before that. I think there's a sense in which we were addressing the last two years.' *When the World Knows Your Name* was definitely, defiantly more blatant in its hopeful optimism than *Raintown* had been, that album's lighter moments sometimes lost within its cooler arrangements.

The single that first informed people of Deacon Blue's new approach was 'Real Gone Kid' which found its way into the shops in October 1988, some six months ahead of the album. It was the first real commercial evidence of just how their army of fans had been swelled by their live work, the first time since their unsuccessful attempt with 'Dignity' that a brand new song, unavailable elsewhere, had been released. The single ascended the charts to reach No. 8, comfortably their best outing, with a *Top of the Pops* appearance the inevitable consequence.

The success of 'Real Gone Kid' must have been a marvellous fillip, an antidote to one of their most depressing moments as a group. Taking time off from recording in August, the band had agreed to play a couple of festival shows, both to take a break and to illustrate the giant strides that they'd made over the course of a year. First of all, they refreshed their political credentials by taking part in a 'A Festival for a Nuclear-Free Scotland', a benefit on behalf of the Campaign for Nuclear Disarmament held at Edinburgh's Meadowbank Stadium on 6 August. They shared the bill with Aswad, Aztec Camera, the Mighty Lemon Drops and Voice of the Beehive. Having been asked to do the show, there was no question of their missing the opportunity for these were exactly the kinds of political engagements that attracted them most, while the CND argument was something close to their hearts. 'He Looks Like Spencer Tracy Now' had indicated their distaste for the strategy of nuclear build-up and its attendant hypocrisy, so they were ideal for the show.

If the show went well, the press was harsher, Alastair McKay calling 'Real Gone Kid' 'a prize turkey', suggesting that Ross 'conducts himself in the manner of a Glaswegian Springsteen but, in truth, he's nearer Paul Young'. Dismissing the group as pop lightweights was one thing but when they got to the Reading Festival, things deteriorated very quickly. The three-day festival held over the August bank holiday weekend has rarely been a haven of peaceful goodwill, with groups that don't fit the fans' demands generally getting a pretty rough deal indeed. The final day, Sunday 28 August, was to be headlined by Squeeze, with Hothouse Flowers second on the bill, Deacon Blue third.

Deacon Blue lasted around five minutes before being hauled off the stage because of fears for their safety. Ross was still plainly shocked a couple of months later when he explained the ordeal to *Record Mirror*. 'It was dreadful, for hours after it was as though we'd all been involved in a car crash. You have to question the audience a lot, you know? Why is it you can do shows elsewhere in perfect peace and harmony and then you get this? There's something very wrong with that place and the people there. Obviously it pissed some people off that we went off after only one song, but we were being bombarded with full bottles of piss and there was no way we could stay on.

'It was like a children's camp mentality and people were trying to tell us it was all good fun, but I hope the festival gets banned because they're letting a bunch of hooligans run riot. Up here you can go to a Celtic-Rangers match with 45,000 people who hate each other and there'll be maybe twenty arrests – it's called social order and proper stewarding. If you expect that sort of behaviour from people, you'll get it.'

Given Ross' quite justifiable and unmistakable bitterness towards the wider rock crowd that Reading represents, the crowd that is pandered to by the music papers, it's tempting to suggest that their determination to have hit singles would have only been strengthened by the desire never again to play festivals which were widely at odds with their own kind of music and image. Certainly, they were delighted to return to the arms of their own fans when they undertook a month-long tour in support of 'Real Gone Kid' which went through October. They were clearly determined to ensure that this would be a major hit and create the freedom and breathing space that they wanted for themselves.

They played a mixture of large and small venues, from the

bigger and more professionally organized universities such as East Anglia and Sheffield to larger theatres such as Preston's Guildhall, the Caird Hall in Dundee and Edinburgh's Playhouse, finishing up at Van Morrison's old stomping ground, the Dominion Theatre in London's Tottenham Court Road. Knives had been sharpened among the press after the Reading fiasco, a number of critics having seen the unfavourable direction of opinion as far as Deacon Blue were concerned.

Jonathan Romney, writing on the Dundee show in *New Musical Express*, pondered, 'What is it about a homecoming gig which brings out the megalomaniac in a man . . . the mild-mannered man you'd expect from his records is skinned down to his vest and transformed into the weedy man's Bruce Springsteen . . . I'd love to have heard them a year ago playing the *Raintown* songs in more muted form, but tonight hardly a song escaped the Barnum and Bailey treatment, complete with colour co-ordinated lightshow and backdrop, dry ice and singalongs. It's an enjoyable show, but the bombast is misplaced . . . still, when the euphoria's passed, perhaps they'll start cultivating a little more tact.'

Andrew Smith covered the show for *Melody Maker*, ending his review with the words, 'In all probability, the key to having a good time with Deacon Blue is not to think. The problem I find is that I have to keep reminding myself not to think, and it shouldn't be like that.' This went against much of what he'd already written, however, having remarked on Deacon Blue's 'abandoned unselfconsciousness', though he did add the rider that 'this added self-assurance has the ability to liberate and irritate almost simultaneously'.

For Smith, Deacon Blue were the original curate's egg, something that others could agree with as the band struggled through a transitional phase prior to the jump to stadium status. 'The problem comes when Ricky Ross tries to convince us he's just a bluesman at heart as on some of the slower songs. It's showbiz again, the gulf between actually believing what you're singing and going through the motions; he blusters and croaks but isn't moved. Lorraine McIntosh is moved, you can tell by the way she flings herself about the stage that she's lost, she's just being there and it's joyous. She's also a prime example of that late-eighties' phenomenon, the backing singer with a better voice than the frontman yet who still gets to do almost nothing.'

Ross recognized McIntosh's potential far more on *When the World Knows Your Name* and it was her vocal part on 'Real Gone Kid' that gave the song its character. It was of course highly apposite that it should be a vivacious woman that captured the song for it was in part about Maria McKee, Lone Justice's electrifying singer who subsequently went on to her own equally satisfying solo career. 'I went to see [Lone Justice] at the Marquee,' Ross recalled. 'I just couldn't believe it. I only saw the last ten minutes and the encores but it was enough to blow me away . . . it was all I like about gigs. Just the idea of Maria's spirit on stage . . . I had this idea of writing a song about someone who was as spirited as Maria McKee. I just thought – if someone's moved you that much and turned you around and sent you home much happier, I'd love to do that. Maybe people do feel that after our gigs, I don't know . . . Some bands you watch and think "that's interesting", others you want to be part of it. Both can be very effective. But it's the communal thing I want to do. The gig's an event people take part in and get blown away . . . But anyway, I thought she was incredible and that was the basic inspiration for the song.'

Ross' views on musical abandon had certainly changed over the course of eighteen months – from worrying at the prospect of having too much of a hold over an audience, he was now relishing the prospect of taking on bigger and bigger crowds, playing better and better shows. This was a view reinforced by the choice of B-side, Hüsker Dü's 'It's Not Funny Anymore'; there being little apparent common ground between the work of Bob Mould and Grant Hart and that of Ricky Ross, he explained the seemingly unlikely selection as a reaction to another key experience.

'I first saw Hüsker Dü three or four years ago in Glasgow

and they were amazing, completely manic. But they also had these brilliant tunes and I stood down the front for about thirty minutes until I couldn't take it any longer. I thought it was great. It's so intense and not something that I could do myself but when I heard "It's Not Funny Anymore" I thought it would be great for someone to cover as a country song or something. It's good to do other people's songs because you learn from them and it also puts out a bit of information about your own musical background, about what you've listened to.'

Ross was not averse to the kudos that such off-the-wall covers bestowed on the band, turning the trick again with a rather unorthodox but very interesting reading of Julian Cope's 'Trampolene' on their next single, 'Wages Day'. 'We're very conscious of wanting to do a variety of things and not succumb to the music business pressure to go just one way, i.e. to go gold, platinum, then double platinum. That's all a lot of people think about, but we like to expose ourselves, do quite a lot of different B-sides, do a lot of different cover versions live.'

Although Ross still maintained that he was trying to do things his own way, Deacon Blue were equally willing to co-operate with CBS, a sensible approach. As 'Real Gone Kid' had been such a success, it was clear that Deacon Blue were about to move onto the next rung of the ladder. From the festival gloom, one salient point emerged in the reviews. Of their Edinburgh performance, Alastair McKay wrote, 'From their inception, Deacon Blue have been a stadium act . . . they're comfortable with the format.' The time had come to take this particular bull by the horns, as Ross accepted.

'I love this word "stadium". I think our next album will be called *Stadium*. What do people actually mean? I've been in clubs in Glasgow which hold 200 people and the performer hasn't managed to get beyond the second row. There's been nothing intimate about it whatsoever. And I've been in Sheffield United Football Club and seen Bruce Springsteen and, you know, my heart turned and I walked out in a different direction.'

Ross was not concerned about concepts of scale, but rather about creating a close, uniquely revelatory atmosphere with the people that had paid their money to see Deacon Blue. 'Intimacy is an art, you create it. It's not an art, it's a craft – as a performer you learn it, how to create moments. You don't do it by appearing at the Marquee and not the Hammersmith Odeon.' Ross added, 'We're more doers than thinkers. We're more about feeling, not completely confessional, but intent on capturing the raw edge of emotions, something very private, perhaps.'

Elevation to the ranks of those few bands able to pack the larger halls was ensured by the second single from *When the World Knows Your Name*, 'Wages Day', released in February 1989 and another top twenty hit, an ideal marketing opportunity a few weeks before the album was released. 'Wages Day' might have found a place on *Raintown* in a different form, perhaps, for it was another song in the tradition of 'Dignity'. Ross was understandably pleased with its success, but far happier with the writing process.

'"Wages Day" is the kind of song I've been trying to write for most of my life. I've been trying to get down to less and less, fewer and fewer chords and words. Like Bruce Springsteen – some of his best work was *Nebraska*, all so economical. I mean, do these epic songs actually achieve anything? You can do it, eventually. It's like Samuel Beckett writing his novel on the front page of the *Guardian*. You can condense everything you're doing.

'Paddy MacAloon, now he basically worries that Bruce Springsteen has one image for life. I love that idea. If I could find one image, if I could find one bloody chord, I would keep it. If I could be like Van Morrison and write *Astral Weeks* in about three or even two, I'd be the happiest man alive! God's truth! Your whole life is about trying to get rid of all the shite. Let's get down to basics here. We like this, we like this, we don't like this, we don't watch *EastEnders*, we don't waste our time with that half-hour, we don't waste our time with F Major 7th, we move on to other things. If somebody said to me "'Wages Day', that was a bit of a single, it was, like, three chords," I think, "Great!! 'Wages Day' is where I want to be."'

Stripping music down to the bare essentials is an interesting concept. For some the skeletal frame wins approbation – David Byrne is a good example. Where Ross took flak was that, although the songs may have been pared down, the production values were souped-up to create the big music, that dread phrase again. The next leap of logic was inevitable – Ross went for musical and lyrical simplicity to ensure that the maximum number of people could catch a glimpse of what he was saying, then the production team of Warne Livesey and Bob Clear-mountain were let loose on the master tapes, building things to a glorious crescendo to fill the great indoors and outdoors with sound.

There's possibly something in that for, placed alongside *Raintown*, *When the World Knows Your Name* was, artistically at least, something of a disappointment. Tracks breezed past you at 100 miles an hour, all glinting in the sunlight. There was little evidence of the impeccable use of light and shade which had made *Raintown* a record to which you could turn time and time again. To be brutal about it, *When the World Knows Your Name* was a collection of very good rock singles that were nice to listen to a few times but had few secrets held within them that would entice listeners to play them over and over again. With *When the World Knows Your Name* what you saw was almost exactly what you got.

Just like *Raintown*, the opening salvo gave the listener a very good idea of what they were about to come across. But if *Raintown* sucked you into its myriad moods, *When the World Knows Your Name* pinned you to the wall. 'Queen of the New Year' was a country and western pastiche of some description, a great singalong concert number and a lyrical departure from what Deacon Blue had previously served up. This was an upbeat love song, an example of things going right for a change rather than the unfortunate misunderstandings and broken hearts of the predecessor. 'Wages Day' and 'Real Gone Kid' were already very familiar songs to any purchaser of the album and so needed no new introduction, carrying the record along at frantic pace before the compulsory ballad took centre stage.

'Love and Regret' was the epitome of stadium rock and everything that that genre has come to represent. Close your eyes and there were 10,000 people holding cigarette lighters in the air in a darkened hall. To dismiss the song so lightly is misleading, perhaps, for it was a classic example of Ross' ability as a peerless balladeer, writer of the bitter-sweet love song *par excellence.* It stood alone to a very large degree on this record which was considerably more upbeat and happier than *Raintown.*

'Circus Lights' characterized a lot of the record with its exemplary musical backing, James Prime taking centre stage with some especially imposing and atmospheric keyboard work, but the first side closed with perhaps the album's finest moment, 'This Changing Light'.

As an idealist and one committed to the idea of his songs actually saying something to people, it was difficult to see quite how he would cope with his new-found status. From a political viewpoint, *Raintown* had had its moments, but in 'This Changing Light', Ross was bitingly savage, tearing into the cruel woman – no prizes for guessing who – that had torn his native Scotland apart with her merciless pursuit of dogmatic ideas. The guitar work from Graeme Kelling was suitably vituperative, with the drama heightened further by Prime's excellent keyboard patterns, Ross' count-down of the years of Thatcherite tyranny being quite chilling.

It highlighted the question of whether a band like Deacon Blue, allegedly so safe and cosy, had any place in dealing with politics and if so, what exactly their role was. 'Wages Day' had, in similar fashion, hinted at broken dreams, not romantic ones but dreams of work, of hope, of escaping poverty, yet all that people seemed to pick up on was the admittedly memorable chorus line, giving it little further thought. The idea that Deacon

Blue were politically radical was given no thought at all beyond Scotland's borders and consequently few thought to look for any deeper meaning to the songs. Many might have sat through 'This Changing Light' waiting patiently for the blast of 'Fergus Sings the Blues' that launched the second side after the beautiful delicacy of 'Sad Loved Girl', a song bracingly free of any sign of bombast.

'Fergus Sings the Blues' was a hugely enjoyable slab of Stax soul with a blistering brass section and another telling contribution from James Prime, rapidly establishing himself as the musical linchpin. His playing notwithstanding, he took co-writing credits on 'Queen of the New Year', 'This Changing Light' and 'Fergus Sings the Blues', giving an additional musical perspective to Ross' more familiar sensibility.

'This World Is Lit by Lightning' was amiable eighties pop without the joyous swing of its immediate predecessor. 'Silhouette' was a nice change of pace, a looser song that made excellent use of Lorraine McIntosh's voice. David Kahne's production – his only credit on the album – suggested that the record might have survived more satisfactorily, if less successfully on a commercial scale, in his capable hands. 'Your Constant Heart' was something new too, with Ross growling like Shane McGowan at times, introducing a much-needed roughness to the proceedings.

'One Hundred Things' proved that absence had not withered Ross' heart to the plight of some of those he'd left behind in Glasgow. It was the story of another loser in terms of the world at large, though it was couched in an incongruously celebratory musical setting. Ross' sensitive portrayal of a down-and-out deserved better, his personal politics being lost in the headlong rush for the end of the song. As though learning from the experience, the most affecting song on the record, 'Orphans', was more subdued and restrained.

Co-written by Ewen Vernal, it was a sad reflection on the way in which Scotland had been transformed over the eighties, leaving it unrecognizable as the country it had been a few years before. Instead of being a vibrant and mutually supportive community, like so many areas of the UK it was now roughly divided up between winners and losers, the inevitable consequence of the race towards a free market. The track was produced by Deacon Blue themselves. It was clearly a song close to their hearts and one which was all the better for their close supervision; they made the right musical decisions. A sparse arrangement left it to close out the record as a lament for a world long gone; a downbeat note on which to close, even if Lorraine McIntosh's vocal was strangely heartwarming and hopeful, ever the Deacon Blue signature. To some, 'Orphans' represented the saving grace of the record, an island of serenity amid music that raged, soared and roared but without the substance to render such pyrotechnics in any way appropriate.

When the World Knows Your Name was released to a great promotional fanfare. It went to No. 1 in the UK album charts in the first week of release, replacing Madonna's *Like a Prayer*, for which many were truly thankful. It sold 300,000 copies in a fortnight and in Scotland it outsold its closest rival by eight to one over that period.

With *When the World Knows Your Name*, Deacon Blue had really arrived. The next question was just what had they let themselves in for, and had such a blatantly commercial move been the right thing for them to do? Ross had achieved his avowed intent of 'going mainstream', but what do you do when you get there?

CHAPTER TEN

Getting the band to the point that John Lennon termed the 'toppermost of the poppermost', it's tempting to think that *When the World Knows Your Name* provided all the answers. Surely it should have defined what Deacon Blue were about while for the band themselves, it should have been the culmination of all the hard work they'd put in over the previous four years, the achievement of all their commercial and artistic goals.

When the World Knows Your Name received a number of positive reviews. Andrew Collins, reviewing it for the *New Musical Express* drew comparisons with *Raintown*. 'Everything about Deacon Blue '89 is bigger and broader and more water-tight. A grown up album . . . [they] walk the line from *Raintown* to Memphis with their heads held high.' Oddly, given the climate of the day and the way in which Deacon Blue were soon to be beaten for this very characteristic, Collins praised them for having made 'a proud and shameless assault on mainstream public consciousness . . . Ricky Ross [is] stirred on to make this wide-eyed, brow-beaten BIG music by his own inability to accept his situation. The recurring theme is "light" (and for "light" read "hope")'. Joining in with some U2-bashing in the wake of *Rattle and Hum*, Collins concluded, 'Deacon Blue will never fly the U2 flag – they're too bemused by the bright lights to come over all standard-bearing . . . This album is great value. Here's to panoramic pop.'

Q, in the shape of Mat Snow, was equally as effusive, awarding four stars, rendering it officially 'excellent'. Harking back to a concert earlier in the year to illustrate their appeal, Snow continued: 'Deacon Blue . . . had a packed London audience on its feet for every minute of a grandstanding three-hour show . . . if only life were so intense, so larger-than-life. There are those among us who think that Mr Ross is a bit of a pranny. But I for one salute his bravura belief in the big sweep, the epic gesture and his attempts, however clumsy, to invest the stuff of everyday romance and recession life with a filmic rock poetry. Though the band lack finesse they stoke excitement efficiently and can drop into a soulful reverie when the song demands it; less grudging praise goes to Ricky Ross' vocal foil, Lorraine McIntosh, who adroitly feminizes the band's texture and so saves us on more than one occasion from being flattened by an excess of overwrought macho chest-beating.'

It was this raucous nature, this stoking of excitement on song after song, that some found the most exhausting feature of the record, with few opportunities for any kind of reflection at all. Snow's most pertinent observation came when suggesting that, 'Though at thirty, Deacon Blue's mainman Ricky Ross is leaving it rather late, you can hear it in every note that he is seizing his moment with a fervour that may never come again.'

It would be an act of unforgivable churlishness to deny such a strong songwriter his moment of glorious breakthrough, but in his desperate attempt to capitalize on *Raintown* it was Ross who was stripping each song of its possibilities. The moments of melancholy which had been so moving on *Raintown* were there but never had the chance to work their way under the listener's skin since they rushed by at such ridiculous speed. Ross had yet to absorb one vital lesson – once you have an audience that is prepared to listen to you, you don't have to shout at them any longer.

It took him a further year to realize his error. 'Up to the

point of making the *When the World Knows Your Name* LP and probably beyond it, we were still touring in student unions and clubs and when you're touring in that situation you still get onstage and wonder if everyone is actually going to stay at the front of the hall. So the idea of playing a concert hall tour where people paid for their tickets and actually stayed to watch, that seemed strange to me. I felt I needed a way of keeping them there.' *When the World Knows Your Name* did have some fine songs on it, but after a couple of plays, you'd lost sight of them as you reached for the eardrops.

You can look at *When the World Knows Your Name* as a record deliberately crafted in such a way as to make concerts a breeze; huge swathes of music designed to fill cavernous halls, cartoon sized chunks of emotion that would appeal to the crowds of thousands that would now flock to see the band's shows. As a careerist move, you might even suggest that it was a sound one. None but Ross knows the truth of this, but it seems fairer to suggest that, as a fan approaching the sorts of concert stages that his idols had trod before him, he simply chose to follow the obvious route, producing Springsteenisms left, right and centre to help carry him through another step into the unknown.

After *Raintown* we wanted to see and hear more about Ricky Ross – we knew all about his influences, we'd all heard *Tunnel of Love*, we'd all seen the Boss in concert, what we wanted was to see Ross shake off the influences and instead of wearing them for all to see, absorb them and allow the real Ross character to come to the fore. There were hints of it happening, but that was all. The time had come for Ricky Ross to inspire the generation following him.

Deacon Blue had never seemed especially concerned with the idea of creating a new form of music and exciting response in that way; their form of inspiration was concerned with ideas, the uplifting aspect of their muse which drew so much criticism and yet which was the at the root of their power over an audience. Graeme Kelling accepted that a wider crowd might have taken some of the wrong messages from *Raintown*, looking at the group as miserablists, asserting that, 'There are two sides to us, that other side seems to have been totally ignored. The songs on *Raintown* are actually really uplifting, there's a joyous aspect to them as well as a description of a certain time and place – and we leave people to make up their own minds about where that it is.'

There was a sense in which Deacon Blue asked for the kind of reaction they got. Oscar Marzaroli's beautifully imposing and characterful photograph of the Glasgow skyline set the tone for many, a point which Ross was quick to take. 'We had the picture for the cover [of *When the World Knows Your Name*], which was reflected street lights on the band. I think it's a great photo, and it was taken in the same street as the cover of *Raintown* but instead of facing out towards Glasgow, it's back in towards the faces. It's a more personal record, more introspective and the cover for me is quite symbolic of the record. You've travelled out, you've done all these things but you end up looking much more back into the place again, back into the people, back into relationships.'

Looking back into relationships had to lead Ross to searching his own soul and drawing on the burgeoning relationship that he and Lorraine McIntosh had – this was the 'getting a good start again' that he spoke of in the wake of his divorce. It would have been easy for this to upset the balance of personalities within the group, animosity rising to the surface among the others, but there appears to have been little internal dissension within the band at any point.

Turning his analytical gaze towards *When the World Knows Your Name*, Graeme Kelling conceded that '[these songs] are even more positive, which is good. I'd hate to be involved in something that was only negative or always super-cynical. There's far too much of that in the charts already. I think the most you can hope for from any song is that it speaks to you and that you can get something from it that you recognize. There are certain things common to everyone's experience and if you're a good songwriter you know what these things are. And I think Ricky is a good songwriter. He's definitely capable of capturing those universal feelings in a way that other people can identify with, and that doesn't seem to be happening too much these days.'

If Ross might have been accused of being maudlin on *Raintown*, *When the World Knows Your Name* wore the broadest of smiles through much of its stately progress. Lorraine McIntosh agreed, saying, 'I think the new songs just seem a lot happier. The first album was a collection of ten years of songs for Ricky. His whole growing-up period was coming out in them and there was a lot he had to get out of his system.'

Naturally enough, Ross concurred with his partner's view, adding, 'Life has changed and things have moved on and it's time to get happy again. A lot of the new songs are optimistic love songs. Where *Raintown* was about adult love and lots of different characters, [*When the World Knows Your Name*] is about coming back down that hill a lot more merry . . . I think a lot of people misunderstood *Raintown*. It wasn't dismal in that sense. There were a lot of positive aspects. But a lot of things weren't achieved. A lot of characters in *Raintown*, things didn't go right for them. There was so much misunderstanding. Disillusion. Discontentment. Where in [*When the World Knows Your Name*], there's a lot of resolution. To me, it's a fiercely loving kind of record. And maybe some of the love comes across as just a joy thing! It'd be great if that happened! I'd love people to take that out of it!

'I think people should always realize that life is bigger than records and you can only take them so far,' he warned, though whether this was to alert the fans to the song's wider meaning or to protect himself from prying eyes was uncertain. 'About the most pretentious thing I ever heard was George Michael saying, "This record sums up the last two years of my life." If I thought I could sum up the last two years of my life in a record, I'd be appalled! His life must have been tediously boring! Records can form soundtracks for people, which is a different thing entirely.

For me, *Tunnel of Love* became the soundtrack for a certain period of my life, to some extent a difficult time but also getting a good start again and I always associate it with that. It seemed to have a lot of echoes of things that were happening to me. *Raintown* is a record of people mismatching and falling out of love, there's a lot of disenchantment, dissatisfaction and struggle there, and disappointment.'

So if *Raintown* wasn't Ross' stab at remaking Phil Collins' *Face Value*, what of *When the World Knows Your Name*? 'If I was trying to get a handle on it, I think there's a fierce falling-in-love on it, but people still aren't fully reconciled. In a song like "Silhouette", it's like a successor to "Chocolate Girl" except the two characters are much closer together. The guy is still a bit of a bastard but they're getting there. On "The World Is Lit by Lightning", they're determined to fall in love, while "Your Constant Heart" is the final resolution! It's an unashamed love song.

'And those songs reflect what was happening to me. In between *Raintown* and the new album, my marriage split up but people don't need to know that, I'm not saying it's important that they're aware of that. You've got to try and write songs from a wider perspective because people in Papua New Guinea or wherever won't necessarily be aware of what's been happening to you and you've still got to make the songs work for them.'

Part of the change in Deacon Blue's approach came about simply because Ross' songs were no longer centred around his vision of Glasgow, although McIntosh countered that even *Raintown* had not been a purely parochial exercise. 'I don't think a lot of *Raintown* was about Glasgow specifically. The Springsteen songs that mean something to me may have been written in New Jersey but that's not just what they're about. They're about the universal things in life that happen anywhere.'

Tongue in cheek, she continued, 'Actually all the [new] songs are about life in Knightsbridge. That and spending the winter in Paris . . . no, they're just about life and love and isn't that what all the best songs are written about?' Certainly for many people, the only hope and warmth that comes into their lives comes through falling in love. The world outside may be cold and difficult to deal with but if you can close the door on it for a while, there is some relief. Deacon Blue's songs delved into that area of life and as such offered hope to their fans. Some saw that as a glib, easy option but when you saw how many people were moved by their records and concerts, it's hard to be disparaging about a group that sheds a little light in the darkness, even if it's for just three minutes or three hours. The light of hope that burned so brightly on *When the World Knows Your Name* was very welcome in many lives, even if a large percentage of the audience simply picked up the album for its bright and shiny things.

America was a problem that they wrestled with too, since they were perfectly open about their desire to break through into that market, the market which any band needs to crack at some stage for the sake of its financial health and longevity, even if the consequences are not always musically appealing. When pressed on the American inflections in his singing voice, Ross went on the defensive, exclaiming, 'It's not intentional. It's just like all the music that I really like, Van Morrison and Elvis Costello, for example. They're the same and they take on board all these influences, that's where it all comes from. Most of the great Scottish and Irish bands have been American-influenced but the important thing is to stay honest on the lyrical side of things. As long as you don't go beyond your understanding and your own framework then you're OK. I mean I'd never write a song about America, I couldn't begin to. That's the biggest trap.'

Even so, the introduction of Bob Clearmountain's American sheen was clearly a record-company attempt to prepare Deacon Blue for the big push on the other side of the Atlantic. When it was explained that they'd actually recorded some of the album in Los Angeles, the die was seemingly cast – Ricky and the gang were bound for the USA. The reality was of course less dramatic, and a grim reflection on the musical infrastructure in Glasgow.

'It's all very nice to go to a place like [Los Angeles] but it's one of the saddest things when you think about it – that in Glasgow we've had so many major pop groups, especially [since 1985] after Simple Minds, and yet you still have to go elsewhere to even mix a track properly.'

Warming to the theme, Ross continued, 'There's hundreds of groups here, management and all that, but no facilities and a lack of the basic skills. We needed a session player for some B-sides and there just isn't that network here that you can plug into so you end up crossing the border just to do wee things. Things are changing a bit now,' maintained the eternal optimist. 'I notice Wet Wet Wet are putting some of their money into a studio and set-up here and they deserve credit for that. We've found a graphic artist from Edinburgh to do all our T-shirts and things, but it's people's attitudes that really offend me. It shouldn't be like this.'

Attitudes in Glasgow had been warming towards Deacon Blue, though. Ross was relieved to be able to say, 'Glasgow's reaction's been amazing, though it also goes without saying that there are many people in town who couldn't care less about us one way or the other . . . Deacon Blue were never the coolest band in town.' Nevertheless, the time had come to turn their gaze beyond the city once more, taking to the road in support of the new album through the city halls of Britain, playing three shows at Hammersmith Odeon and another at the Aston Villa Leisure Centre in Birmingham.

Reactions were seldom less than ecstatic, with good reason. 'One of the things we've always tried to do as regards the shows is to do things from a fan's point of view,' Ross told *Hot Press* in May 1989. 'I'm thirty-one years old, I know what it's like to be a fan, I know what it's like to have queued up for tickets. I know what it's like to be into a band and to want to get more of the music, which is why we put extra tracks on B-sides and do things which show another side to us. We try to do things which I feel are the right things. I don't mean by playing a huge media game but in the small details, I think they're the things that are important and in the long term, they're the things people remember you for.'

Over the course of the tour, Deacon Blue rarely played for less than three hours, ripping up stages the length and breadth of the country. By the end of the year, they had made the transition to the largest venues in the land, closing their most commercially successful year to date with a series of arena shows, 'Fergus Sings the Blues', 'Love and Regret' and 'Queen of the New Year' all having made their presence felt in the singles charts. Writing in *Melody Maker*, Ian Gittins said of the Wembley Arena show, 'This was a triumph, proof positive Deacon Blue can cut it in the major league. This was intimate. Deacon Blue have mastered stadiums.' He noted that they were 'engaged in a struggle to transfer their smooth melodies and pounding songs to stadium size . . . gaucheness and rawness under a slick façade'. Yet, 'Lots of odd things happen. Deacon Blue are more peculiar than you think.'

Others were taken aback by the sheer power that they exhibited. *Hot Press* had remarked on the album's 'metallic reserve' and this harshness was translated into live performance. Of the SECC show, *Record Mirror* concluded, 'Gone is the sensitivity of *Raintown*, its torched melancholy magic dumped unceremoniously in favour of the easy way out, the BIG route to BIG success . . . [Ross] hardly even had to sing to 'Dignity' as they played what felt like the twenty-four-inch spectacular with ten minutes of pure stadium pomp, half of which consisted of an anything but dignified auto-pilot while Ricky went along the line namechecking the band. I'm sorry but the only thing I could think of was the curtain call at the end of a pantomime. That might seem a bit harsh – what they do they do better than anyone else – it's just that what they used to do, and what they will do, is really so much better.'

It was not an entirely isolated opinion but by this stage, Deacon Blue's immediate future was already mapped out for them, with 1990 set to feature a number of mega-gigs. There were signs in the live shows that this treadmill was starting to wear away at the core of the band, a situation that would have to be addressed as soon as possible in order to protect that spirit. Possible solutions suggested themselves in the activities that the band indulged in away from the full glare of publicity, including a reawakening of a more overt political commitment and a brush with the TV industry.

CHAPTER ELEVEN

Over the course of his career, Ricky Ross has clearly if inadvertently demonstrated the very different agendas that control the three constituent parts of the music industry beyond the artist himself; the press, the company and the public. The seeds of those differences as far as Ross is concerned were sown from the time he became a singer in front of a band.

The press are concerned with great music and excellent performances, it's true, but they are also governed by trends and the need to appear well ahead of their time in order to protect their status as arbiters of public taste, ahead of the musical game rather than reflecting it. Of necessity then the press must take a rather jaundiced view of established acts, sneering at their popularity. By this stage, though, the artist no longer requires the patronage of the press for they have found their own musical constituency – the fans.

The fans are, for most groups, a central consideration. As far as Deacon Blue were concerned, they had carefully nurtured and built up a fanatically devoted fan base who admired their down to earth, unpretentious performance and attractive popular songs. In return for their cash, Deacon Blue provided them with that greatest of assets, the quality most likely to win loyalty: value for money – long shows, singles with new songs, long albums, the works. By trying not to take the fans for granted, Deacon Blue were able to remain sure of their commitment. It's only fans who want value for money: after all, reviewers and record company employees don't have to pay to get in and so prefer a short show giving more time in the pub.

The third outside party is the record company and it is here that things get complex. Without keeping the record company happy, you don't get the chance to make records. Sometimes you have to commercialize yourselves further than you would choose. By the close of 1989, Deacon Blue were very close to that point.

To maintain their own interest and to ensure that they kept their feet on the ground, they had engaged themselves in political issues once more. In 1989 public opinion was galvanized in response to the implementation of the poll tax. Demonstrations and marches were held, public meetings called as people protested at the prospective legislation which was to eventually be the downfall of Margaret Thatcher.

Edinburgh was the scene of a major rally against this pernicious piece of law, following which many of Scotland's major bands played a benefit concert at the Usher Hall. Deacon Blue were among those present, Lorraine McIntosh making a point of stressing their political sensibilities. 'There's lots of political things which the band would love to get involved in, whether they're charity gigs or just out to make a point but we're rarely free to do them. It was great to do the [Edinburgh] gig about something that everyone in Scotland feels so strongly about. We wanted to make our attitude to the whole thing known.' From the stage, Ross rallied the crowd, encouraging their protest.

Not only were Deacon Blue very sensitive to this particular issue – Ross proclaiming that he was going to refuse to pay his poll tax during the course of a brief but barnstorming set – but it was also a release for them to return to doing what they had set out to do. This was not a question of popularity, of market penetration, of aiming for particular cultural groupings or any other piece of marketing jargon. The Edinburgh gig was an example of the band making their music, enjoying it to the full and making a serious point at the same time.

Ross had spoken of his aims in that direction prior to taking *When the World Knows Your Name* on tour. Reflecting on the group's position in the big league, he noted, 'I like the fact I can get my own way [with a crowd]. Say what I want, do what I want. Have a channel to do that in,' yet some of the celebratory stadium rock connotations did concern him. 'That's called triumphalism, isn't it? Nobody wants it. I always worry about it. Any gig which has emotional overcharge has the danger of doing that. It's very much up to bands how they deal with it. We've had this thing, where fans turn up like, "Hey, we're the boys!" I think then you've got to sort of say, "Look, we're dealing with serious issues here." Take the thing off on another track. I'm very conscious of this coming up to our next tour. I don't want to spoil people's fun. But it'd be good to channel some of the things we do.'

Much given to this kind of statement, he would then insist on extolling the virtues of a fun night out, which rather ruined his radical chic, Ross enthusing that 'certain things have to be larger than life. I think there's a huge entertainment factor in music. Some things are blown up, humorous on a stage. Others are stated more obviously. Or more subtly. Just so the point can be made. In the days of videos and large cinema-style screens, being on stage is slightly old-fashioned. So certain basic things have to be kept alive from the vaudeville days.'

The political content, contrary to wider opinion, had not gone out of Deacon Blue's music, though it had been obscured perhaps by the surface brightness. Nevertheless, Ross was still a committed socialist, increasingly nationalist in view. 'Orphans' and more especially 'This Changing Light' had shown that he still cared passionately about Scotland. A keen student of history, he was able to contrast the curse of apathy that was politically strangling the United Kingdom as a whole, notably Scotland itself, with the proud legacy that the Scots can boast as many of them rushed to join the International Brigade to fight the evils of fascism during the Spanish Civil War of the 1930s.

'["This Changing Light"] was literally written on the way back from Spain,' Ross explained. 'The Spanish-Glasgow connection suddenly occurred to me as I was trying to find a way of dealing with the last ten years and what's happened to Scottish people. The basic statement in the lyric, for kids who are seventeen or eighteen years old who buy the album, is that I want you to know that this place you're living in is utterly changed, utterly. Our expectations for school-leavers today and the expectations that people had ten years ago are just completely different. If somebody had told me ten years ago that the National Health Service would be run down, I literally would have laughed. If they'd told me that water was going to be for sale I would have fallen off the chair! It's sickening!'

Scotland has a very difficult position with regard to its democratic voice compared with the rest of the United Kingdom. Given seventy-two seats in Westminster's House of Commons, the country regularly returns barely a handful of Conservatives. As the country votes for the Scottish Nationalist Party or the Labour Party, the Conservatives have little interest in its affairs, apart from a little scaremongering at election time. As a nation, Scotland has suffered as badly as anywhere from the destruction of the nation's industrial base.

Scotland's problem is that since 1979 it has voted for a government that it doesn't get. The Scottish conundrum is whether anti-government protestors should rally behind Labour or the SNP. If they vote SNP, they will obviously never get a majority in the House. Even with seventy-two MPs, a Conservative government could still ignore their voice and their arguments for independence. Additionally, in voting SNP, they are reducing the number of Labour seats, thus making a Conservative victory more likely. If they vote Labour, however, even if Labour were to take power – something that has eluded them on four consecutive occasions to the bitter chagrin of the Scots – they might only offer Scotland its own assembly rather than real executive power over taxation and legislation.

In the days of poll tax, this was an especially sensitive issue, so the SNP were fortunate that a by-election was held in Govan, Glasgow, in November 1988. A Labour majority of 19,500 – the seventeenth safest seat in Parliament – was overturned by the charismatic figure of Jim Sillars, himself a former Labour MP. Basing his campaign on a relentless assault on what he termed 'Labour's feeble fifty', a reference to their fifty MPs in Scotland, he indicted them as being complicit in the collapse of Scottish industry and for failing to fight the poll tax properly. Sillars' slogan of 'an independent Scotland in Europe' proved powerful, though the Labour leadership was heavily criticized for what Tony Benn called 'a reflection of our failure to discuss constitutional questions which are at the core of the devolution argument . . . it revealed that if you don't offer people analysis they go for separatism'.

Ross was in complete agreement as far as Labour's inadequacies went, and he was by now a fully paid-up nationalist. At the Edinburgh show he introduced a song directly inspired by that by-election, 'Don't Let the Teardrops Start', recalling it as the last time Scotland was happy. He was quick to point out that, 'A lot of people are asking very nationalist questions such as if we were separate, if we had our own parliament, if we could raise our own taxation, our own legislation then perhaps we could represent what people actually want. The SNP are starting to answer some of those questions – these are huge constitutional questions, but certainly people here are voting one way and they're getting the opposite policies, so something has to give.'

Ross' determination to continue hitting political issues head on was exemplified in June 1990 when the band headlined Glasgow's Big Day, a celebration of the city's position as European City of Culture. Before a crowd of around a quarter of a million, Ross attacked the government's recent decision to close the Ravenscraig steel plant with the attendant massive job losses while also standing up for a country 'sold down the river by the Labour Party in Scotland'.

Ross had shown political ambition back in 1987 as *Raintown* was released. 'What I think is important is that the biggest band in the world right now are U2 and they're not going around sticking needles in their arms or bonking everyone in the northern hemisphere. Instead they're gigging and their singer is going down to Central America and, by so doing, alienating half of his potential market and I think that can't be bad. I've seen all the big bands but I've never seen a band willing to do that. I think bands should get behind people who haven't got a voice, not just necessarily give money to causes. That was what was frustrating about Band Aid. It didn't change people's ideas about spending on Third World development. Two years after Band Aid, we have a general election and no one is asking what any party's policy on Third World development is.'

There was a sense in all these proclamations that Ross had developed a way of working that suited his needs, giving himself the freedom to be controversial, to be political if he felt so moved. Of the Big Day, he remarked, 'I made a "political" statement [there] which landed me in the soup and which I won't take back. It's healthy every so often to say, "We're pissed off at this and angry about that."' Here was the Ross that many of his admirers wanted to see, giving free rein to his instincts rather than being hidebound by convention. Yet in the next breath, he poured cold water on those hopes, recalling all those comments that he was simply too polite and reasonable to be a rock star.

Talking to the *Glasgow Herald*, he said, 'Big political statements from pop stars are null and void, worthless, stupid. Pop stars shouldn't do it. We were offered the Kurdistan debacle (organized by the shy, retiring Jeffrey Archer) and I'm glad we didn't do it. If you're going to give money, fine, give it. But if you stand up and say something at a pop concert, people just think, "Ah, there's somebody standing up and saying something at a pop concert." It's unhealthy and it's being done for the wrong reasons. Sales figures went up after Live Aid and no manager has ever forgotten it.

'The Big Day was good in that its organizers were honest . . . it was a civic knees-up. But big events can be dangerous. Concerts should be about fun, enlightenment, moments of joy that suddenly come to you on the way home. They shouldn't be a big deal.'

That hint of cynicism reflected a pop star who had perhaps been pushed a little further than he would have liked and required to do things that were not to his taste. That aiming towards some kind of transcendent moment in a gig was a worthwhile, laudable ambition but surely such moments came from nowhere – placing political restrictions on yourself was not necessarily the best way to go about finding them.

Musically, Deacon Blue were looking to move away from the limelight to re-establish just why they were involved in the pop business in the first place. An opportunity for this reassessment came from the unlikely source of playwright William McIlvanney, author of *The Big Man*. The group were asked to take part in his play, *Dreaming*, scheduled for transmission on BBC2 in the spring of 1991 though the initial invitation had come towards the end of 1989. Described as a satirical comedy, the play followed a seventeen-year-old who fantasized about meeting his heroes, Deacon Blue.

This led to an interesting collaboration between the band and McIlvanney who had prepared four sets of lyrics for the group to work with. Between them they worked on these songs, 'Love You Say', 'Let Your Hearts Be Troubled', 'Is It Cold Beneath the Hill?' and 'Killing the Blues', readying them for broadcast. This provided a nice change of pace for the group.

Director Mike Alexander was delighted with the results, telling David Belcher of the *Glasgow Herald*, 'Everything fitted perfectly. It came at the right time for the band who were off the road, resting in the middle of a tour. Most important Ricky and Willie got on very well.' Ross was equally pleased, fired up by the challenge of writing with someone new and for the different medium of television. 'I had to know if Willie was happy for me to work a little on his lyrics too . . . we met, discussed things and he was happy enough . . . I found the idea of doing a musical a bit funny, because you tend to think of Julie Andrews and people suddenly bursting into song for no good reason. But *Dreaming* uses the songs in different ways, in different settings which work well.' Deacon Blue declared themselves delighted with the way things had progressed. 'I was told "never do music for films" by Jon Kelly who produced our first LP . . . he told me, "The music you think is the best will always get cut out of the finished film . . . it'll be frustrating."'

On the contrary, the band were only too happy to get back to playing music for the fun of it, though normal service was to be resumed in September 1990 when they returned to the stages of the UK, playing multiple concerts at venues such as the Aberdeen Exhibition Centre, Wembley Arena and Birmingham's National Exhibition Centre. The impetus for this run of concerts was the release of *Ooh Las Vegas*, a perfect example of just how far record company ambition and the group's best interests had diverged.

As far as the band were concerned, *Ooh Las Vegas* was a collection of odds and ends aimed squarely at the fan's market. Boasting twenty-three songs, it looked reasonable value for money again, but there were a couple of drawbacks. Firstly, it was in part a rounding up of B-sides that the more fanatical members of the support would already have in their collection. But in order to entice those people into buying the record too, CBS threw in a handful of unreleased songs including those from the *Dreaming* soundtrack, though this was mitigated by the fact that the double album sold for the price of a single LP. Stir in a full-blooded promotional campaign and *Ooh Las Vegas*, far from being the low-key filler record that it was intended to be by the band, became another bloated statement from some bloated rockers.

The musical environment had changed in the previous year with the Happy Mondays and Stone Roses filling the pages of the weekly press and a hardening of attitudes towards the likes of Deacon Blue. In a savage review, Terry Staunton from the *New Musical Express* gave the album two out of ten, dismissing it with 'life's too short to listen to twenty-three Deacon Blue songs. *Ooh Las Vegas* is one of the most unnecessary records ever released,' although this was some improvement on another review of the band which simply said, 'Let's face it. They're crap.' More objectively, it was hard to argue with Staunton's rage at CBS's marketing techniques: '*Ooh Las Vegas* is actually the band's second ragbag of loose change. In the brown-nosing sleevenotes the A & R director of CBS says it was the idea of "some bright spark in the marketing department". One wonders if this was the same "bright spark" who came up with the idea of repackaging Deacon Blue's debut LP *Raintown* with a limited edition LP of out-takes and B-sides thus forcing the band's biggest fans to buy *Raintown* twice. It's a typically deplorable move that we've come to expect from record companies.'

Select was in broad, if rather more kindly, agreement, calling it 'a very tiring exercise. The unpalatable truth is that this music is exactly what you'd expect – more of the same, but not as good'. Given the fact that *Q* had put *When the World Knows Your Name* in its top fifty list for 1989, they were a little happier with the compilation, conceding, 'Deacon Blue, being genuinely prolific, can justify this kind of outlet for its tastier leftovers,' while *Vox* gave it eight out of ten, surprisingly so since the review was little given to praise. 'It takes a certain amount of arrogance to release what is basically a B-side retrospective album only three albums into your musical career . . . if nothing else they're to be congratulated for sheer gall . . . *Ooh Las Vegas* is a premature album and one which benefits existing fans rather than attracts new ones. But when you're a hugely successful band with a captivated audience, who gives a toss?'

By this stage, CBS had been taken over by Sony Music. Ross was suitably horrified by the company's behaviour, recalling later: 'The worst career move we made was releasing [*Ooh Las Vegas*]. I dislike pretension and it was intended as populism –

we just wanted to bang it out there, in the way the Smiths had done with *Hatful of Hollow*, but it got misconstrued. We got such a lot of flak for that album, and not surprising, really. The Smiths doing that kind of thing with Rough Trade is one thing; Deacon Blue doing it with Sony is quite another. You can't present an album to Sony without them going, "Right, we're going to get this fucker in the charts!" Great. The sales guys are really brilliant. I feel closest to them of all the people from the company that I meet; they really support the band and want your stuff to be successful. But that wasn't the game plan on this occasion; it was just a junk collection of songs that might be interesting for fans. It was not a new album. In retrospect we'd probably have been better just letting it filter out through the bootleg network.'

The storm that raged over *Ooh Las Vegas* blinded people to its charms. It was an unassuming collection, relaxed and consequently highly enjoyable. Without the throat-shredding forcedness of *When the World Knows Your Name*, it sported a few fascinating cover versions such as 'Trampolene', the *Dreaming* tracks, which were intriguing, and a couple of lovely pop tunes 'That Country (Beneath Your Skin)' and 'S.H.A.R.O.N.'. Ross did his best Tom Waits impressions on 'Gentle Teardrops'; the Govan celebration, 'Don't Let the Teardrops Start', was there and the album was notable too for 'Ronnie Spector', taken from the band's original CBS demo session. However, the big sell, added to which were the big gigs, simply overwhelmed the inevitably slight nature of some of the tracks.

The simplicity and enjoyment that existed on *Ooh Las Vegas* should have been a pointer for Ross and the gang to calm things down, to relax and let the music take care of itself. However, pre-planning had checked them into the biggest arenas, carrying them right back to the big sound of *When the World Knows Your Name*.

With the Deacon Blue backlash in full swing, there was plenty of scope for the poison pens. One reviewer noted, 'Too often throughout the show the band ramble on with extended versions of their best tunes, making for an exceedingly dreary and self-indulgent evening . . . not a lot happened here tonight.' *Sounds* on the other hand were able to admit that the 'complete lack of cynicism does enable Deacon Blue to put on a refreshingly soulful performance', acclaiming the 'undeniably perfect pop of "Chocolate Girl" while Ricky looks suitably embarrassed as cheers greet him shedding his jacket . . . Deacon Blue offer a lightweight soul package, the innocence of which is both its appeal and its weakness'. *Melody Maker* were a little less convinced, though, accusing the band of being 'nice to the point of nausea . . . after two hours they leave you with an overriding sense of nothingness, like opening a gift box to find it empty inside. And that's what's so offensive about Deacon Blue.'

At least some reviewers were grudgingly able to concede that, even if Deacon Blue were not precisely their cup of tea, the audience was having a whale of time – with more than 60,000 tickets sold for the English shows alone, popularity was not an issue. The 'quality' papers were now taking an interest in the band too, though their journalism was no more objective than the music press'. Commenting for *The Times*, Jasper Rees wrote, 'Evidence suggests that Deacon Blue have dedicated themselves to putting the "l" back into "band" . . . soulless songs about roots, romance and rain . . . it laid bare the paucity of the musical imagination.'

Caroline Sullivan was more perceptive and therefore more interesting. 'Ricky Ross' perception of this band as master craftsmen in the elegant Steely Dan tradition is at distinct variance with his fans' notion of them as pleasant Radio 1-esque balladmongers . . . to the non-partisan, Deacon Blue are neither, but purveyors of mildly diverting mid-tempo sophistisoul . . . [The horn section] by rendering them inaudible neutralized Deacon Blue's strengths, the lyrics and Lorraine McIntosh. Ross is the nominal leader but Lorraine, backing vocalist and tambourine hitter, is the Deak you watched.'

Ms Sullivan was particularly taken with Lorraine McIntosh's work, asking once again why she didn't take a greater share of the vocals. Were she to get the chance, 'Deacon Blue could be one of the pop sounds of the nineties,' she opined. Earlier in the year, *Melody Maker* had said that live, Deacon Blue were 'the Ricky and Lorraine show. Nobody else matters, they may as well be session men' and there was a great deal of sense in that. Perhaps it was inevitable, since the two married in the early part of 1990, that they would be closer on stage and, as the two main singers in the band, attention naturally gravitated towards them, especially to Lorraine McIntosh, who provided the only femininity in what was becoming a quite macho sound.

She had little time for the record company celebrity makeover team. 'I'm quite insulted actually that I haven't [been approached by the company stylists],' she complained. 'They've probably written me off. "There's no way we're going to make her look good, so we won't even try."' It's more likely that she and the band warned the company off trying to spruce up their personal image. 'Someone in a review said that I came on stage looking the spit of Just William in my shorts and Doc Martens, then some feminists came up to me after a gig in Bath and said they felt I was being used as the token sex object!'

Image was something that clearly did concern the group, though. Invigorated by their extracurricular activity earlier in the year, Deacon Blue tried to take a fresh approach to their work and in August 1990 brought out an EP called, logically enough, *Extended Play*. It contained covers of four Bacharach and David songs, a logical return to Ross' songwriting inspiration and a flirtation with the fun side of making records once again, though it was a recording session instigated by James Prime. 'The record company were completely bemused,' remembered Ross, Prime adding, 'People said it was a clever marketing idea but we were simply enjoying our success.' Therein lay the real problem with Deacon Blue, one that would eventually wear them down. With a track record like theirs at CBS, no matter what they did, however light-heartedly they took it, people saw it as part of a marketing masterplan. It was ultimately to prove an insurmountable problem for them.

CHAPTER TWELVE

It's not always easy to stoke up a great deal of sympathy for a band that claims it's been misunderstood when it has happily sold millions of records across the country.

Even so, on a personal level, Ross and company had clearly been forced to go through a fairly miserable twelve months in the aftermath of *When the World Knows Your Name*. Playing concerts in cavernous halls that were built for boxing matches or basketball games amid a hail of increasingly aggressive criticism isn't always a bundle of laughs and while the money might compensate, any songwriter or musician always craves a little credit for their work.

Dougie Vipond remembered discussions 'between various members over a bottle of whisky late at night when you feel like you're getting things out of your system but you wake up the next morning and they're still there'. As the Deacon Blue juggernaut got bigger and bigger some of the wheels started to work loose.

Ross was perhaps regarded as the architect of some of the problems, inasmuch as he was the main songwriter and it was his change of style and emphasis towards this huge, inclusive sound that had given birth to the songs that were gradually grinding the band down. James Prime noted that, 'Ricky likes instinctive things, songs that are rough and ready, warts and all – it doesn't't matter as long as they're fresh,' though that obviously wasn't the way the band were playing it. There may well have been a hint of professional jealousy in the wake of the media concentration on the 'Ricky and Lorraine' aspect of the band, particularly after they had got married and became a kosher rock 'n' roll couple.

From a musical point of view Ross manfully shouldered some of the blame. Remembering the process of making that record, he said, 'Everybody wanted us to make an impact with the second album and my thinking got very confused . . . We were pushing it to go very rock 'n' roll and we were pushing it to go very pop. In the end we just lost cohesion . . . The whole thing was geared to being harder sounding, more poppy, more radio-orientated. The playing was compromised by this desire to impress. Too much time was taken up in searching for sounds rather than thinking about songs. We were very affected by other bands, wanting to show we'd covered the ground in the hope that so-and-so would pick up this influence or that.

'It just wasn't focused. And the most frustrating thing was that it wasn't really what I wanted to do . . . The record did really well. People bought it and we became a rocky, singles sort of band – bright sounding young things! – but the magical side of our first album, *Raintown*, somehow that was missing . . . a lot of the time during that last album I would come into the studio and feel, "Well, I don't really like this but I have to go along with it," and I think we all felt that way. The recording of the LP had ended up strung up over a whole year because we were touring so much and because the producer fell ill. Even the original title of the album, *Ooh Las Vegas*, ended up getting lost somewhere along the way in America. So we ended up not even having a title, we didn't have a running order. All the things I like to have, they just weren't there.'

Having brazenly set their sights on world domination, Deacon Blue were soon to discover that the world wasn't actually very interested, the only consolation coming from some Pythonesque looking on the bright side of life. Ross noted,

'We were at home one day and Lorraine said that maybe it wasn't such a bad thing that we didn't break America with an album which, frankly, we had both gone off. So let's make a great album next time and if we hit with that at least it will be something we can honestly stand over.' With the exception of reasonable success in Spain, club gigs were on the agenda elsewhere, paradoxically providing a welcome respite in the change of pace.

The much-vaunted idea of getting a band sound had failed to reap rewards too. Vipond argued, 'After *When the World Knows Your Name*, I think the whole band felt it was much stronger because we all had more input, but after listening to it, we realized it wasn't a band album at all, it was everybody throwing in things trying to create a space, trying to get their own bit to be remembered by, and that was so wrong.' It was part of a natural progression that culminated in *Fellow Hoodlums* where everyone felt that they knew one another properly at last. 'I think [it's] far more assertive and confident as a result,' claimed Graeme Kelling. 'There's a very healthy exchange of ideas whenever a song comes up and occasionally it can get quite heated. Someone wants to go in one direction, Ricky wants to go in another but eventually it ends up sounding like Deacon Blue anyway.'

The year 1989/90 was characterized by the big gig, an SECC show being captured on video as *The Big Picture* and released in time for Christmas 1990. According to *Q*, 'Sceptics might learn a lot about the mechanics of transforming fine brushwork to the broad sweep needed to make an impact on the big canvas . . . Ross and the other half, Lorraine McIntosh, are the Bruce and Patti of Glasgow . . . she provides some much-needed love interest to an otherwise rugged rock machine.' If Mat Snow was in the business of handing out bouquets, a few brick-bats were called for too as he noted the debilitating effect that arenas were having on Deacon Blue. 'Flatulence is their vice . . . Deacon Blue offer terrific value for money, true, but sometimes more means less.'

If they had embraced the idea of 'stadium rock' with a naïve enthusiasm at the start of 1989, the reality of it all was rather disappointing, chipping away at the group's enjoyment and resolve. Presenting music of which they had lost sight to appreciative crowds for the first time at Wembley was one thing, the excitement of the occasion carrying everyone through, but residencies in these unforgiving stadia were another thing entirely. By the end of that year of promotion and touring, Ross 'thought I might quit. It took a year of horrible vibes before we could all finally sit down and have a soul-searching conversation. Then we came out and said, "Look, this is shite. What are we gonna do about it?"'

The response of the group as a whole was to agree to put marketing concerns behind them, ignore the idea of tailoring their sound for bigger and bigger markets and get back to playing the music that had so inspired them in their formative years, the kind of songs that had made them want to form bands in the first place. Surprisingly in some ways, the first response was to go back into the studio and enjoy messing around with a few cover versions. 'For the first time ever, and after all the things we'd planned on the world dominating tours hadn't happened, here was something we all wanted to do which was just fun. I'd been listening to some old Petula Clark stuff and thinking, "there's nothing wrong with any of that."'

Most interestingly, Ross was finally coming to terms with his own goals, distinct from those of his record company. Accepting that taking the world's markets by the scruff of the neck was neither as easy as had seemed likely, nor perhaps as vital, he admitted to himself that the music was more important. Having a triple-platinum selling album under his belt, he was now materially secure and Sony would be unlikely to drop him; as Ross himself had said, 'Hits guarantee your longevity. All you want as a working musician is a record that's going to take you through to making the next one. And if you can get three or four songs on the album that the record company think are hit singles, then they won't fuss.'

Like many a musician before him, Ross had been forced to compromise his art for financial security. In the aftermath of *When the World Knows Your Name*, however, he took a long look at himself and realized the foolishness of what he had been trying to do. The most sensible approach for his personal well being and self-respect was to please himself, make the best records that he could and then let the record company get on with the job of selling them. Having so decided, Ross awoke one morning to find himself a free man as far as his musical interests went. He could now give his instincts free rein once more.

There was certainly no desire in the band to repeat the formula of 'Real Gone Kid' which had preceded *When the World Knows Your Name* and become a radio fixture. Ross said that as far as singles went, 'You can only choose from what's available. Yes, of course the Americans would love it if we delivered a single like Sinead O'Connor's ['Nothing Compares 2 U'] for instance and if we had a song like that I wouldn't complain! It would certainly solve any financial problems. But the downside of that would be to dwarf the album with a giant single – that's why I've always liked Beatles albums, there's a strength in depth from beginning to end.'

Ross was clear about his disaffection with *When the World Knows Your Name*. 'I would be pleased if people heard *Raintown*. I would certainly be pleased if they heard *Fellow Hoodlums*. I wouldn't disown the second record but I just feel it's not the record I would like to be remembered by, but unfortunately a lot of people . . . heard songs like 'Real Gone Kid' and 'Fergus Sings the Blues' and identified Deacon Blue with songs of that ilk, thereby missing out on songs such as 'Orphans', 'Town to be Blamed' and 'Raintown', songs of a darker nature with perhaps more space.' Dougie Vipond was in agreement, for in dismissing *When the World Knows Your Name*, he asserted, 'I think for me "Orphans" was the one hang-over from *Raintown*, spirit-wise. It was the one saving grace for me.'

'What we are, I now realize, is a lyrical, melodic, songy kind of band,' Ross reflected to *Q*. 'And the song is a very flexible kind of thing. It's not just like a bunch of people who sit on a groove and then come up with some catchy stuff to lay on top of it. It doesn't matter whether you crank the guitars up to whatever or whether the snare sounds like a pistol shot. Production hasn't got anything to do with it. What matters is the song, and that you're really caught up in the playing of it. You could take a washboard and still make it work. I'm firmly convinced of that.'

When the Bacharach and David EP was revealed to the world in August 1990, the band's intuition proved wholly correct. By simply being themselves, relaxed and enjoying the songs, they had their biggest hit single, which reached No. 2 in the charts. The four songs, 'I'll Never Fall In Love Again', 'The Look of Love', 'Message to Michael' and 'Are You There (With Another Girl)' were among Deacon Blue's best recordings so far. It was rather appropriate that they were kept from the No. 1 spot by a piece of novelty marketing, the timeless Bombalurina reaching the summit with 'Itsy Bitsy Teeny Weeny Yellow Polka Dot Bikini'.

Resolve suitably stiffened by having been proved right in their new approach, Deacon Blue embarked on their third album, which was to be released under the banner *Fellow Hoodlums*, much of which was recorded in Paris though it was finished in their traditional habitat, Glasgow's Cava Studios. Keen to break free of the over-ornamentation that had ruined *When the World Knows Your Name* with its emphasis on production values, the band turned again to Jon Kelly who had produced *Raintown* so successfully. Ross was especially happy with the change, noting: '*Raintown* certainly contained elements that the last album didn't, a little bit of looseness, a little bit of space. Jon says that what we have – which a lot of bands find it hard to create – is emptiness and space. On the last album we found that space and clotted it all up again. But I don't think we'll make that mistake again . . . Jon just likes people to enjoy playing; he has a great way of letting you express yourself and he's very disarming. I said to him once, "Aren't you worried about the hiss on this keyboard?" and he said, "How many modern recordings have you got at home with hiss on them?" That shut me up.'

The new attitude of fun and musical enjoyment created the best possible atmosphere in the studio, the album being written and recorded between November 1990 and February 1991. Lorraine McIntosh remembered the sessions fondly, saying, 'We were in Paris and everyone was playing this new song in the studio, live, and it was just some of the best times we'd had all year. I mean, you don't think about it. You don't think, "Will this be a hit single?" or "What will this be like at a gig?" You're so into what you're doing, you don't care.'

Ross suggested that, 'This was the not-at-all difficult and thoroughly enjoyable third album. This was a piece of piss.' This was in part helped by the strict discipline he imposed on himself in preparing to make the record. Once *Ooh Las Vegas* had been released, Ross took two months off for planning and writing. 'There were lots of little bits of paper lying around, little ideas for lyrics and songs . . . I wanted to sit down, get them typed up and actually review what I was doing. And the result was that in December when I walked into the studio, I could hand everyone sheets of lyrics and feel, "We really know where we're going here." Because when you're not ready and prepared for something, that's when things can take a wrong turn.'

Banishing any record company advice from the studio, the band simply got on with making music, a technique which had served them so well when making *Raintown*. Demos were a thing of the past too, the unsuccessful transition from there to the finished product on *When the World Knows Your Name* still a painful memory. Ross accepted that 'I felt they had killed off a lot of the spontaneity in there'.

His songwriting methods had of necessity changed, since he no longer had the time that had been available when he built up the backlog of songs from which *Raintown* was selected. 'I used to write songs in an empty room with a piano and a tape recorder. I could spend the day working on a song and then spend a couple of days recording it after that. I haven't had a day like that for ages. And because songwriting is something I just have to do, even aside from commercial considerations, I now find myself humming tunes into walkmans and doing things on the hoof that I wouldn't have done before. I'm starting to get to play guitar a bit more and I've started carrying an acoustic guitar around with me – the whole writing songs on the back of the bus trip! Very rock 'n' roll!'

Nevertheless, this development was a welcome one, encouraging a musical simplicity and a return to more acoustic instrumentation. It was something they'd dabbled with in live performance where the group played a brief acoustic set to bring down the tempo. This and the absence of synthesizers immediately gave the new songs a lighter feel, room in which to breathe. *Fellow Hoodlums* is an LP made for its own sake. All the decisions about it were based on music, not 'we want to be living in big houses in ten years time', Ross told the *Glasgow Herald*. 'I get annoyed with bands who disavow their first eight LPs, but I'm uncomfortable with our second LP and while I was happy at the time with the first one, now it's too technological for me. *Fellow Hoodlums* is a natural no-click-track, non-sampled-drums record. It isn't horn-rimmed boffins poring over manuals.'

There was an almost poetic lyricism to much of the music that flowed effortlessly from the album, some of their early influences being distilled into their own blend of music while new musical flavours were also tried with regularity. The most obvious sense that *Fellow Hoodlums* gave the listener was of the unrestrained joy that the group got from making it.

With this new record, Ross retreated back to the Glasgow that he knew, yet was still exploring. The album was filled with place names and phrases redolent of the city and happily free of any patronizing edge. Ross was quick to acknowledge that he was still something of an outsider even in his adopted city. 'There are Scottish names that are magical and interesting, bits of Scottish language that are fun,' Ross conceded. 'Lots of people in music are outsiders, skulky people. That's definitely me. I think of myself as a songwriter, which is behind the thing a little bit. I can't think of myself as the singer and I resent the fact that I've ended up doing it. It's a shame that the star system means the singer gets to be known. Nevertheless, I still feel an outsider in Glasgow. I'm still discovering the city. The Glasgow I know and like and understand provides a natural backdrop, a time and a logic, for the characters in the songs. I can't see them elsewhere. But it's important that people in Aberdeen or Delaware aren't put off. It's not important to know or like Glasgow. This LP is simple basic human stuff that transcends any barrier and it will.'

'Someone listening to the album in Dublin, for example, can still appreciate the music and the songs for themselves, which are basically love songs,' Ross insisted with some justification. 'When I was growing up I didn't know much about the American place names on records but it certainly didn't impair my enjoyment of the music; in fact some of the places mentioned took on a mythical status. Besides it's nice for Glasgow remembering also that names can bring colour and magic to a song.'

Ross' Glasgow cropped up again and again in the songs and accusations were levied that here was a middle-class boy from out of town trying to wrap himself in the clothes of working-class culture. Was it a case of Ross tiring of Springsteen and attempting instead to take on John Lennon's mantle? 'Definitely not . . . I'm not from that background [and] I'm not into that working-class hero thing. The themes on this record are more universal. I've used Glasgow as a metaphor for life with its lights and shade, beauty and ugliness. So in "Your Swaying Arms" for instance, Kelvin Way becomes Heaven.' This was nothing new for Ross, though. 'In fact, I've always imagined my songs being set somewhere. "Chocolate Girl" from the first album is set in certain streets, I just never mentioned them.'

His affection for Glasgow and the determination to leave an indelible mark on its culture through *Fellow Hoodlums* was rekindled by his work for the Oscar Marzaroli trust. Marzaroli had taken the cover photograph for *Raintown* but had of course built up an enormous reputation for himself over many years for his intimate portrayals of working-class Glasgow through his photography, his legacy being a powerful piece of social documentary.

Marzaroli, like Ross, was not a native of Glasgow, but came to the city in the 1930s as a child when his parents emigrated from Italy. Ross was installed as a trustee of the Oscar Marzaroli Trust, founded on his death and dedicated to his work. Its principal aims were to set up a gallery to show his pictures, along with studio and workshop facilities to encourage young Glaswegian photographers. Ross' workload often meant that he was unable to attend meetings and so in mitigation, he organized the compilation 'The Tree and the Bird and the Fish and the Bell' to benefit the trust. The record featured contributions from Deacon Blue, Wet Wet Wet, John Martyn, Lloyd Cole, the Blue Nile and Eddi Reader, among others.

To carry on the tradition, the band looked into their own backyard when deciding on the sleeve for *Fellow Hoodlums*. Glasgow had its own flourishing school of painters through the 1980s, featuring such talent as Peter Howson and Ken Currie, Howson having most recently come to wider attention as the official war artist in Bosnia, his dramatic paintings having attracted acclaim and denouncement in equal measure. The method of these two men was to use huge canvases, populating them with human grotesques, struggling to survive amid urban decay. There were echoes of the work of such eighteenth-century artists as Hogarth in the social documentation inherent in their work, Marina Vaizey noting in the *Sunday Times* that Peter Howson's 'portraits are mostly of dossers, Howson's neighbours at a church refuge and of people of the night in the streets and in the clubs. The feelings are contradictory; of life forces long since spent or pent up and bursting still with unquenchable vigour'.

Ross drew some inspiration from the same well and his own songs had much of that character about them even if his own personal compassion refused to allow him to use such grotesque caricatures in his work. However, the artwork provided by 'Central Design/Bridges & Woods' gave a clue to the music contained within and was a handy point of reference for potential purchasers. As an aside, the work was given its own exhibition at Kelvingrove Art Gallery and Museum in May 1992. Using the work as both a piece of art and a commercial for Deacon Blue, the exhibition followed 'The Story of an Album Campaign', including a range of design material.

Once past the sleeve, the music was the richest mix of styles that the band had ever placed before its audience. 'James Joyce Soles' opened with a cascade of strings that owed much to the Nelson Riddle Orchestra, the whole song returning to the cinematic wash that had been so important to *Raintown*. The invocation of James Joyce was an interesting one, suggesting perhaps that *Fellow Hoodlums* was an ambitious attempt at a 'Glaswegian *Ulysses*' as *Hot Press* remarked.

Ross felt the use of strings was important, recalling, 'In Randy Newman's case strings are used to highlight and underpin some of the darker more malevolent aspects of his songs like "Sail Away", a song about slave trading, or "Birmingham", a song about racism, so I've attempted to use strings in a similar fashion.' There was a brooding quality to the track: as the first song on side one made perfectly clear, Deacon Blue were mining different musical and lyrical territory this time around, though it dovetailed neatly with 'Orphans', the last track on the previous album, which had also closed with an uplifting vocal coda from Lorraine McIntosh.

That brief reference to 'Orphans' was particularly telling, for it was that song which had given the new album a direction. '"Orphans" was the one glimmer at the end of the tunnel for me,' said Ross of *When the World Knows Your Name*. 'I remember that Ewen and I had been in the little studio downstairs [at Cava] and we'd done that track in just one day and it was really "Deacon Blue" . . . Jon Kelly has just started using this phrase a lot – "what is and what isn't Deacon Blue?"

It hadn't really occurred to me that we sounded like a certain thing, that there could be a Deacon Blue sound, but I think there is and I think it's summed up on "Orphans".'

'Fellow Hoodlums' itself was almost a travelogue of a trip around Glasgow's darker, vibrant streets, with Ross singing as if he was in another room, great big gaps being left within the song, a skeletal bass figure pushing things along in its own time. Their decision to play a more minimal kind of music was wholly justified by the strength it gave to songs like this, which allowed the listener's imagination free rein, but it was also a reminder of battles previously lost.

The song 'Fellow Hoodlums' proved to be a cornerstone for the rest of the album. '[It's] a nostalgia song about a guy in Glasgow and it caused two things to happen. First the lyrics suggested a whole lot of other ideas – little things about Glasgow, incidents which might become songs – and I suddenly found I was getting back to being really happy here. Happy in this town, happy writing about it and getting deeper and deeper into the place and the relationships here. I didn't want to just skirt round the city or view it from a long way off, I wanted to get right under the buildings . . . set the songs right in there amongst all the ebb and flow of it.

'The second thing that happened with the "Hoodlums" track was that I found myself really struck by the arrangement: I started to hear the things that I liked about Richard Thompson's records in the seventies. The simplicity of it. A guitar, a bass, a drum, a vocal. I thought, "When I go out to make this record, I want it to sound like that."'

The palpable sense of relief that came from the record provided a relaxed atmosphere in which the group were able to work without constraint, producing a song like 'The Wildness' which was a return to their Celtic influences as personified by the music of Van Morrison. Lorraine McIntosh was also allowed her first lead vocal on 'Cover From the Sky', which was released as a single eventually. Typical of the Deacon Blue school of crescendo-creating, hers was an impressive performance though it did lead the track into MOR territory and as such was one of the less exciting pieces on the record.

'[We're] letting the music breathe,' reflected Ross. 'Oddly, that was a criticism we got early on – "there's huge gaps". So we spent time filling them in, making happening, bubbly little demos that wouldn't lose A & R men's attention.' The spacious arrangements that the group excelled in on *Fellow Hoodlums* were a delight, creating a more manageable music that people could live with and explore further. It was a record where new things presented themselves on each listening, while the intriguing lyrics and odd musical juxtapositions meant that there was a far higher boredom threshold than had been the case with the crash, bang, wallop of much of *When the World Knows Your Name*. Ross was more confident as a lyricist, Deacon Blue more accomplished as a band.

The Glaswegian feel was most pronounced on 'The Day That Jackie Jumped the Jail', a rough and ready number coloured by an abrasive guitar, with a chorus that was akin to something by the Cowboy Junkies at a drunken party. An old-fashioned bluesy rocker, it highlighted just how well Deacon Blue worked as an ensemble force. It came across as a riotous mixture of seaminess and the wild elixir of freedom – maybe a metaphor for their own change of direction. Again there was a sense of hope in there, not in the heavy handed way of days of yore but in a more human context that was much more enjoyable in consequence. There was a hint there too that Ross' work with William McIlvanney had opened his eyes to the wider lyrical possibilities that stretched out before him, the characters being explored fully, if explosively.

The lead single for the album was 'Your Swaying Arms' and was a warning shot to those who expected another head-on assault from Glasgow's own Hit Factory. A cooler single than we had been used to hitherto, it still boasted a huge chorus and was classic Deacon Blue in some respects, while it remained quite understated and free of any bombast. Ross accepted the point, adding, 'We don't feel the need to bang people over the head with what we do, we want people to enjoy Deacon Blue in their own time, at their own pace, in their own way and when people are given that opportunity they tend to appreciate it more rather than having been assaulted by a massive marketing campaign. Also, it's important not to let people unfamiliar with the band feel excluded, and I would say the whole album is in keeping with this approach.' Low key it was, reaching No. 23 in the charts.

Lorraine McIntosh agreed with the thinking behind it, saying that, 'We want people to listen to our albums as a whole and not just us as a singles band, hence our decision to release "Your Swaying Arms" as a first single instead of the more radio-friendly "Twist and Shout".' She was right on that account for 'Twist and Shout' reached the top ten on release, but more interestingly it was characteristic of the material on the second half of the record.

'Twist and Shout' itself was an almost cajun work-out, taking influences from world music via Paul Simon and David Byrne. This was no surprise since side two opened with the soft jazz-rock of Pat Metheney in 'A Brighter Star Than You Will Shine' which featured some excellent work from Dougie Vipond, and was set to embrace Latin rhythms in 'One Day I'll Go Walking'. 'Closing Time', a late-night chucking out song, was built around a huge slab of Sly Stone funk guitar, and dabbled in Philadelphia soul before time was finally called. There were suggestions of Deacon Blue hopping aboard the Madchester bandwagon at this late stage but Ross dismissed them. 'We're aware of what's happening and it's nice for cheeky young bands to come along and stick two fingers up at the likes of us. It's a healthy thing but I don't feel the need to reciprocate,' said Ross when challenged. 'I wouldn't denigrate anyone for what they do. In fact, I like the Happy Mondays singles, it's a refreshing change to hear some good dance music as opposed to the Stock, Aitken and Waterman type.'

As *Fellow Hoodlums* proved, Ross had clearly lost none of his talent for wordsmithery, creating a range of poignant or humorous vignettes from urban life, stories brought out all the more by the seemingly contradictory musical backing. One song which sat outside these boundaries, though, was the deeply moving 'Goodnight Jamsie', a proud, swirling tribute to Lorraine McIntosh's father who had died the year before. Ross remembered, 'I suppose he was my father-in-law although me and Lorraine weren't married at the time. I just felt very close to him. He was a really big character, a larger than life character. He used to come to the gigs and everyone in the crowd knew he was around.'

The restrained manner in which Ross tackled such delicate subject matter amply illustrated just how far he and the band had come over the course of *Fellow Hoodlums*, his partnership with James Prime extending both to the full. It was Ross' first attempt at such directness, as he admitted. 'To be honest, I shy away from writing songs for or about people I know. I would hate to be the singer-songwriter people avoided, you know, "Keep well clear of him or he'll write a song about you," but with Lorraine's father, I always felt he was the type of person you could write a song for, who would be really pleased. There will be nobody happier in Heaven now than him. In fact, Lorraine's brother wrote what I think is a better song about him called "The Big Club" and when his dad heard it, he used to walk about the house singing the song about himself!

'He was a great man, a special person and his sudden death had a huge impact on me and obviously Lorraine who was devastated, and for me, being with someone you love who is grief-stricken is something not to be forgotten. Jamsie's death, and its effects on Lorraine and myself, finds its echo in a lot of this album.'

There were hints of that loss within the music, most obviously in 'I Will See You Tomorrow', but it was not a album of mourning, rather a celebration of the indomitable nature of the human spirit and of life itself, almost a rebirth. In its return to the communal spirit of *Raintown*, *Fellow Hoodlums* was saying that 'We're all in this together, we're all trying to make a living and that if you want to be an artist, you have to work out ways of doing that too.' As musings on the things which make life worthwhile, even if these are moments snatched at in passing, *Fellow Hoodlums* stood as a fitting tribute.

Of course, Deacon Blue's perception of the record and of themselves was rather different to that of the outside world. Ross persisted with the claim that, 'I don't think we are established, we certainly aren't known as mainstream abroad and we've a long way to go yet in terms of the success of established bands' before grudgingly conceding, 'The way it works in Britain is as soon as you have a hit album or a hit something, you immediately become old hat.'

If the critics had been fully justified in attacking the stadium stance of Deacon Blue's most recent live shows, they were wrong not to approach *Fellow Hoodlums* with a more open mind. Adam Sweeting, writing for the *Guardian*, appeared more interested in his reputation than that of the group, accusing them of concocting 'a strange hybrid of mid-western hard rock and Hibernian whimsy, a kind of Jock Kerouac', a line which owed more to his desire to be a (failed) stand-up comic than any reflection on songs which had long since left that hard rock behind. Sweeting continued by saying the album was 'polished and painstaking' which was again a comment to apply to the previous record, suggesting that 'Ronnie Ross [sic] is only a skilful songwriter-impersonator'. While this was a claim that could have been carried with justification two years earlier, Ross had learned to consume his influences rather more than before, so that we were now getting closer to the real man at last. Condemning Lorraine McIntosh's voice as a 'sqeaking wail [which] is one of the most horrible sounds on record', Sweeting came across as a herd-following hack with a hatchet rather than an objective reviewer with a mind of his own. *Select* joined in the game by running a review from two years earlier saying 'it's stadium fodder and all around the world people will add this to U2's *The Joshua Tree* and Dire Straits' *Brothers In Arms*.'

At the other end of the scale, *Vox* reviewer Craig McLean

accepted the album as 'the sound of re-evaluation . . . in few places are proceedings as full of themselves and their own importance as previous offerings . . . the production is husky, deliberately avoiding clarity and precision. This, coupled with lyrics chock full of references to dear old Glasgow, will do Deacon Blue no favours when it comes to packing an arena in downtown Barcelona. But for the rest of us, *Hoodlums* will do nicely, thank you.'

Rob Beattie in *Q* had also taken sufficient interest to listen to the album before passing judgment. He remarked that there was a 'lot of genuine cleverness in the material and the playing – as evidenced by "Your Swaying Arms" . . . which features an unbearably catchy bass line from man of the match Ewen Vernal – and a long, slow dance-hall fade during which Ross and Lorraine McIntosh bill and coo at each other in a manner only husbands and wives can get away with. Just.'

Beattie went on, 'This is an album full of rich contrasts . . . by the time "The Wildness" has come and gone, it's clear that *Fellow Hoodlums* is a record of high quality . . . In fact, it's smiles all round for *Fellow Hoodlums* which manages to balance Deacon Blue's conviction that real people are worth writing about with the kind of pop sensibility that hit albums are made of.'

Certainly, it was hard to disagree that on balance, *Fellow Hoodlums* was Deacon Blue's finest forty-five minutes to date, relegating *When the World Knows Your Name* to the back of the rack. The greatest question that now required a solution was, while they liked it, what would the legions of fans who'd bought the previous album make of it? Initial reports were encouraging, the album entering the chart at No. 2 and sales went on to attain healthy proportions. However, feeling back at the record company ranch was that sales had suffered because of the group's approach.

Live performance was to prove that Deacon Blue didn't much care. Choosing to play multiple dates at theatres across the country rather than a handful of dates at stadiums like Wembley Arena, this version of back to basics was not a panic measure since an equal quantity of tickets were sold, if over more shows. This was the final dismantling of the huge Deacon Blue roadshow that had been carefully built by CBS and Sony in the previous four years.

Ross was unequivocal about the reasons for the change, even though his language might have alienated many of the group's fans. 'The word "stadium" has haunted me. I don't want to play these places. If you do two nights at the SECC or Wembley, you find that your friends don't really want to go. Friends in Manchester who started off with us at the Boardwalk don't want to go to G-Mex. And you talk to them after big shows and you can see it in their eyes, they haven't liked it.

'You look out at big audiences and think, "Who are these people?" They're a mystery to me. Twenty-five per cent of the crowd at any big show – at Wembley Arena, the SECC, the NEC – show up for everything. For Chris de Burgh, us, Shirley Bassey. It's people who buy whatever chart music is prominently displayed in record shops or at petrol stations, and I'm not being patronizing because I buy music at petrol stations.

'The SECC is dead as a rock 'n' roll venue. It's wrong, it has to be knocked down. I like the people there and the dressing rooms are very nice, but if I write an intimate record like *Fellow Hoodlums*, about life and death and birth, I don't want to do it in a big barn over a hotdog stand with the sound bouncing around and people shouting "whoopee!" There must be a way to do big shows, maybe in the open air like the Big Day. You'd get aggro from people who couldn't get tickets if you played in smaller venues . . . but better that than the ones who love us not being there.'

If Ross was scathing about the venues that they'd been playing, it had a hollow ring to it in the light of his absolute commitment to the idea eighteen months earlier when *When the World Knows Your Name* was skilfully piloted into those very arenas. To his credit, Ross had been big enough to admit to his mistake, but asking for sympathy was a little dangerous. Equally dangerous, heretical almost, were his views on the live set, though to outsiders this was a bold and impressive gesture. 'Anyone coming to see Deacon Blue play "Real Gone Kid", "Fergus Sings the Blues" and "Queen of the New Year" will be disappointed in the immediate future. We've played those songs for three years and we'll play them again at some stage; they're lyrically entertaining songs that work well live, but they're not going to intrigue people.'

Fellow Hoodlums was written with just that purpose in mind, intriguing songs that could grow with the audience, songs that didn't come clean on the first hearing. The next challenge was to see just how those songs worked in the new venues and just how kindly an audience would take to not hearing the old favourites that they'd bought not so long ago.

Attending the Hammersmith Odeon, Alan Jackson of *The Times* was suitably fascinated by Ross' 'salt and vinegar lyrics'. Continuing in generally positive vein, Jackson added that, 'It is Ross' force of personality and sense of theatre which dominate. He succeeds admirably in bringing the atmosphere of Glasgow . . . to a west London audience punch drunk on tales of small people surviving in the big city.' The *Glasgow Herald* was equally positive, Peter Easton covering the Royal Concert Hall show.

'Previous unkind thoughts about Deacon Blue have centred on accusations of blandness and . . . an attempt to camouflage [Ross'] over-literate lyrics beneath a rock star pose. Well on this night we can wrap those doubts in a Springsteen poster and float them down the Clyde . . . Deacon Blue are proving themselves to be one of the best live acts around. The two frontpersons who are sometimes guilty of forcing it, let their theatricality loose in a natural flow, gaining strength from a band that sounds exactly right in this surprisingly intimate venue . . . This is not a stadium band and it doesn't need to be.'

CHAPTER THIRTEEN

With ***Fellow Hoodlums*** out and out about, 1992 was spent doing further live gigs in various parts of the world, meeting with varying degrees of success, and writing and recording their fourth real studio album. On a personal level, Lorraine gave birth to her and Ricky's first child in the summer, the group necessarily stepping off the treadmill for the sake of the health of the prospective mother and baby.

There must have been a sense of considerable disappointment in the camp that the group's strenuous efforts to change from their hollow musicality of 1989/90 into a much richer and warmer form by 1991 had met with such little comment. Though some reviewers applauded their courage and the results, the broad sweep of media opinion was that Deacon Blue were the same group. Meanwhile, their level of popularity had declined somewhat with erstwhile fans not taking kindly to the speedy dumping of the hit formula, though their sales were still such that any number of bands would have gladly traded places with them. Sony's reaction is not a matter of public record but it's not difficult to surmise that one or two brows were furrowed in corporate corridors, with schemes being planned to return the band to their glory (for 'glory' read 'lucrative') days.

Deacon Blue had of course been down this path before. They were no longer the naive recording artists that they had been back in 1988 when stadiums, hit singles and the BIG music all seemed such enticing ambitions to be fulfilled. A little more world-weary by now, the thirty-five-year-old Ross was especially determined to follow his own inclinations. Career aspirations became less central to him as family life and responsibilities took on a greater role, though it was to appear that he was increasingly concerned with the state of the wider world.

Encouraged on a personal level by *Fellow Hoodlums*, Ross was determined to follow his own interests and tastes still further in tandem with the rest of the band. Dougie Vipond agreed with the move, saying, '[It's] a risk we've felt is a necessary one. We've become a bit stifled by our past and feel now is the time to really push out the boundaries and see what we're capable of.' New music had been absorbing Ross' attention through 1991 and into the New Year, particularly that of the Stone Roses, Happy Mondays and Primal Scream. The indie-dance phenomenon held echoes of classic acts from the past such as the Rolling Stones, Hendrix and Sly Stone, taking those influences and turning them inside out to create possibly the most influential musical movement since punk.

Certainly their work created an environment where simple, straight classic rock music was no longer enough. Pretty soon, throughout 1991 and beyond, even the great heavyweights such as U2 and INXS were finding themselves pushed towards the dance floor with varying degrees of success – with INXS, it might even be suggested that their career was revitalized with songs such as 'Taste It' giving them the energy to go on into the new decade.

Herein lay the dilemma for Ross. Having spent the last year recharting Deacon Blue towards rockier territory, dismissing the pop game as one in which he no longer chose to indulge, the concept of 'rock music' suddenly began to look outmoded and outdated. The broad consensus seemed to be that all the great songs had already been written, the great albums made and so music needed to go somewhere else. Even Bono of U2, the most successful rock 'n' roller in the world in 1989, was forced to retreat with his band to 'dream it up again'. His response was to say, 'Why would anyone want to buy a record any more? You've got to give people something more now.' Deacon Blue were required to either move with the times or steadfastly stick by a past that they had only just disowned.

The question of whether Ross was a talented songwriter working in a classic tradition or simply a magpie making away with other people's gold has been debated elsewhere. It's closer to the mark to suggest that having started out by wearing his influences on his sleeve, Ross was now revealing more of himself. It would be harsh indeed to suggest that Bobby Gillespie of Primal Scream or the Mondays' Shaun Ryder could give him any lessons in absorbing songwriting influences, but it would be difficult to argue that they had a greater degree of success in creating a more original sound from old sources.

Though the Happy Mondays themselves might argue strenuously against the thesis, much of the credit for their transformation from vaguely interesting rock group to riders of the dance wave could be laid at the door of the Perfecto production team, Paul Oakenfold and Steve Osborne, who overhauled their sound. Oakenfold in particular became *the* face of the dance/rave scene of the time. That being the case, maybe it was not so surprising that Deacon Blue approached the pair to work with them on their new record in order to try and radically shake up their comfortable working practices. From the outside, it was perhaps even more surprising that the Perfectos took up the challenge for it was a move unlikely to do an enormous amount for their own credibility within fiercely fashionable indie circles.

Early examples of their work together were undeniably intriguing. 'Your Town' was released in November 1992 and sounded unlike anything that the band had ever released before. 'Your Town' carried a genuine anger, Ross vocals twisted and distorted to such a pitch that he was almost entirely unrecognizable from his previous records, presumably the intention.

The song suggested musically that comments the group had

made on the importance of the band ethic were not simply empty words, for Deacon Blue sounded like a powerful rock band working towards a common goal. Graeme Kelling's guitar was especially prominent on the track, further out in the mix than had been the previous convention, but all the better for it. 'Your Town' reached No. 14 in the charts, an improvement on 'Your Swaying Arms', the first track lifted from *Fellow Hoodlums*, signifying a degree of acceptance for this new stance which veered idiosyncratically between Fleetwood Mac and out and out madcap dancery.

'Your Town' acted as a good sounding-board for the album to come, a record that was openly aggressive without descending into straightforward rock posturing. Its effect on their following was not as dramatic as it might have been, for such a radical rethink had prompted questions about how open-minded their fan base was. Sony expected it to be conservative, and it is a recurring problem within rock music when a band tries to shake off its past. Having lost some fans with *Fellow Hoodlums*, the record company were not keen to drop any more.

When it was eventually released in March 1993, *Whatever You Say, Say Nothing* caused a few ripples in the musical pond. Deacon Blue supporters fell into two camps; those who hated the new dance craze, enjoyed classic rock *à la* Clapton, Elton and Simply Red and wanted the group to stay within that format; and those who had picked up on *Raintown* early on, or on *Fellow Hoodlums* and appreciated a band that was willing to experiment, push back the barriers of its music and follow its instincts. The second group, however, were smaller in number than the first and *Whatever You Say, Say Nothing* was a comparative commercial failure, even though it reached No. 4 and clocked up another gold record with sales in excess of 100,000; hardly a breadline figure.

In fairness to those that decided against buying it, *Whatever You Say, Say Nothing* was a mixed bag but it did include some of the best work that Deacon Blue had done such as 'Peace & Jobs & Freedom' and 'Fall So Freely Down'. But once again, the old questions of influence were trotted out – was Ross just jumping on a bandwagon to keep his career afloat? A moment's thought would have dispelled that idea since he and the band had been responsible for one of the biggest-selling albums of the late eighties. If all that Ross was concerned about was sales he could easily have dusted down that *When the World Knows Your Name* model once more and laughed all the way to the bank.

Thus *Whatever You Say, Say Nothing* could only be construed as another step in the band's artistic evolution. It was undoubtedly an attempt to recapture some of the youthful excitement of making music for fun since it dripped with references to the late sixties and early seventies, the time when the group were growing up and getting into music seriously. As a trip down memory lane it worked well, especially as it was spiced up by the Perfecto production to give it a far more contemporary feel than might have been the case.

Even so, a song like 'Cut Lip' emphasized the importance of the right image. The song was deliberately rooted in the Rolling Stones' sound, coming on like 'Have You Seen Your Mother Baby, Standing In the Shadow', a piano-driven rocker with hints of the Family Stone. This was a harsher, dirtier affair than Deacon Blue's previously pristine work might have led you to expect, grounded in the music of the moment but it was dismissed out of hand by both critics and public, wary of what might be yet another piece of marketing trickery conjured up by Deacon Blue's record company. Yet within twelve months, Primal Scream issued *Give Out But Don't Give Up* which was filled with souped-up Rolling Stones and Funkadelic riffs – that too made a thoroughly enjoyable album but Bobby Gillespie's wasted charm made it a favourite with the critics because he was living the record, assimilating both the music and the lifestyle. Ross on the other hand was supposedly a clean-cut lad who couldn't possibly understand the music he was making.

Whatever the truth, Deacon Blue certainly played it as if they meant it. 'Will We Be Lovers' came straight out of the Madchester revolution with choppy funk guitars and a darting drum track that propelled it into the charts on its single release. 'Fall So Freely Down' which followed it on the album was a powerful combination of Deacon Blue's traditional virtue – the enormous chorus – and some tricksy discordant guitar work that Happy Mondays had pioneered. The closing section was especially strong, Ross defiantly wailing away into the distance calling to mind both INXS and the Beatles.

There were other sides to this new, slimmed-down Deacon Blue though. Stretching back to the birth of rock 'n' roll, 'Last Night I Dreamed of Henry Thomas' invoked the old bluesman amid a delightful tune, Ross' ear for melody not letting him down, although the use of a crackly old Thomas record in the background reeked of cliché even if it was an attempt at some kind of homage. Almost like a history lesson in classic rock music, the sublime era of sixties pop got a look in on 'Hang Your Head', a track that somehow never received a single release. Again a piece that could have comfortably found a home on the acclaimed Primal Scream record, it gloried in lashings of melodic guitar, Graeme Kelling having a more conspicuous effect on this album than on any other Deacon Blue outing.

'Only Tender Love' allowed him to dabble in harmonics that sounded like a quote from the U2 songbook though the solid thump of Vipond's drums took the song onto a different tack, Ross' voice coming faltering through the ether as if disguised by an alcoholic haze. U2 comparisons held up on 'Bethlehem's Gate' which was Bonoish in approach and content, while 'Peace & Jobs & Freedom' free-wheeled down the M6 to Manchester once again.

Musically, *Whatever You Say, Say Nothing* was a radical departure if possibly not quite the enormous leap into the unknown that both band and producers had envisaged. Oakenfold and Osborne felt that Deacon Blue themselves were holding back the process of change. 'With Deacon Blue it was trial-and-error,' Paul Oakenfold noted. 'We thought we could take this pop group, give them attitude, a new direction and a totally new sound. They were stand-offish, like, "We're the band, we know what we want." I wanted the album to go down one road and they wanted it to go another, it ended up down the middle. I think that album could have been better, but then again it sold really well.' Where it scored was in Ross' performance and the lyrical content.

Taking his theme from the massive changes that the world had gone through in the previous five years, Ross appeared to be distanced from the chaos that was going on around him, struggling to maintain any perspective on his life and relationships. His vocals were generally treated in some way, hiding inside the mix; he no longer made his proclamations from the top as before. This was a record that explored his own confusion and insecurity. There was a political edge to the songs that had rarely been explored so fully or aggressively, with songs like 'Cut Lip' having a caustic savagery to them, attacking simultaneously the manufactured poverty now rife in Britain and the sanitized, mind-numbing television that has robbed people of the capacity to think for themselves. 'Peace & Jobs & Freedom' spoke of a desire to aspire to those important goals rather than pander to a world of commercial greed, looking at the negation of the human spirit that modern life has fostered, attacking the political apathy that surrounds the democratic process. Calling for a return to real human values, it acted as a battle-cry for the album.

The closing track on the record, 'All Over the World', seemed like a revisit of Dylan's 'The Times They Are A-Changin'', though here there was a nagging sense of doubt behind the brave words of hope, Ross' quest for new language, new statements of peace and freedom both a hopeful and hopeless one; for as borders were coming down all over Europe, new ones were springing up in their place. There was also a hint of his religious background in his wait for the new century, since the earliest groupings of the Brethren founded their beliefs on millenarianism, the hope for the Second Coming at the millennium. If Ross wasn't advocating his own belief in that philosophy, he did use the new century as a metaphor for a new beginning.

Whatever You Say, Say Nothing, came across like a veiled attack on soundbite politics and was a strong body of songs, although they did suffer from the considerable drawback of coming out after U2 had covered similar musical and lyrical territory in *Achtung Baby* and as interest in the dance scene was finally beginning to wane. *Vox* accepted that, 'Whatever their detractors have said about them, it's always been clear that Deacon Blue are triers . . . the decision to work with the ultra-cool Perfecto team – an open invitation for yet another music press burying – is proof enough of that.' Having laid down those ground-rules, Alan Jackson went on to say, 'This is an astonishing piece of reinvention by Britain's least fashionable band . . . best of all, new era Deacon Blue sounds almost completely unselfconscious, a first in itself.' This was true – Ross sounded like a man in a hurry, with points to make and not enough time to make them.

Further political proof came in September 1993 when he joined the pressure group Scotland United in their attempt to raise cash to fund a referendum on Scotland's constitutional future. Its chairwoman, Bernadette Malone, noted, 'For the Tories in Scotland, the democratic deficit simply refuses to disappear. We must force them to listen to the will of the people.' Ross was in clear agreement and there seemed little question that the anger shown on *Whatever You Say, Say Nothing* came as a result of the Conservative victory in the April 1992 General Election.

Vox provided a lone voice, though. *Q* savaged the record: '"Your Town" . . . sounded great in clubs and the prospect seemed to be that Deacon Blue had done a Primal Scream and turned themselves, Zelig-like, from a rather lumpy rock band into dance demons. Alas, that song aside, little has changed . . . Frankly, it's a cock-up . . . on more than one song, Simple Minds' *Alive & Kicking* seems to be just around the next verse . . . This album just isn't happening.'

It would be a rabid Deacon Blue fan indeed who claimed it as a perfect album, but those criticisms held little water, concerning themselves with a perception of the group that had been formed in 1989 and took no notice of 1993's realities. Whether you liked the record or not – and in fairness, many didn't – to simply ignore it as being more of the same was lazy and inaccurate. The *Glasgow Herald* was a little closer to the mark, if just as unimpressed: '[The album] openly signalled a clueless leap aboard a dance-rock bandwagon that had sho' nuff done gone left town two years previous . . . Ricky, remember: as well as being unashamedly sticky-fingered, real pop is nimble, up to the minute, quick to spot an opening.'

Where a less well-disposed reviewer might have found some additional mileage was in the album's determinedly retro stance. Even if the Stone Roses et al. had cleverly updated the sounds and the riffs of 1968, they were still from 1968: while genuine innovators like The Edge from U2 were trying to find a new vocabulary, others were hanging grimly from the old and Deacon Blue were guilty of that too. Enjoyably diverting as it may have been, *Whatever You Say, Say Nothing* was saying nothing new about the rock beast, just about Deacon Blue's interpretation of it.

It was the supporting concerts that began to call into question Deacon Blue's hold on what they were doing. The album suggested that the group might choose to pump out a sweaty funk show, leaving behind any theatrical pretensions, just playing the new songs and whatever old material might fit. Instead, again playing multiple shows in medium-sized venues, the group approached rock theatre head on. In the wake of U2's Zoo TV, the concert presentation had become a thorny issue leaving many bands uncertain how to approach a format that had been systematically dismantled.

Writing for the *Glasgow Herald*, David Belcher was stoically unimpressed. 'Is [Ross] brave, foolish or arrogant?' he asked. 'Critics scoff, panning Ricky's glaring leap from Springsteenian singlet to Bono-style lurex and the Deacies' abandonment of anthemic stadium rock for ambient stadium rock. Critics scorn Ricky's parody of Bono's parody of rock excess: two parodies cancel each other out, no? . . . Whatever you say, say something original.' Whatever Ross' thinking was, the appropriation of Bono's finery was a dumb move, an irony that was lost on the majority of people.

The staging left David Sinclair of *The Times* unimpressed too when he caught the show at the Clapham Grand, a warm-up show for the tour proper. 'The lighting now revealed a two-tier stage partitioned by sheets of corrugated iron. Ross and the guitarists patrolled the front ground-floor area, while elevated in the background were keyboards, drums and backing vocalist, Lorraine McIntosh, a sparring partner who clearly knows her place.' While U2-copyist accusations rent the air, Ross responded by saying the show had been inspired by Tom Waits' *Big Time* film, an admission which Belcher felt 'diminished Deacon Blue even further.'

The live shows left the dichotomy at the heart of Deacon Blue cruelly exposed. Did they want to follow U2 and Springsteen to the football stadiums of the world after they had already had one highly unpleasant brush with stadium life? Or were they motivated by a desire simply to make good records in an idiosyncratic style while destined to simultaneously lose their core audience and fail to replenish the fan-base, since those that might have been attracted to the new Deacon Blue were never informed of their existence by a press machine that was too sickened by earlier CBS tactics to give the band a fresh start and a fair hearing?

Rumours began to circulate that all was not as it should be within the band and when a tour scheduled for November 1993 was postponed until the following Spring, apparently due to recording commitments, the vultures began to circle. No new recordings were forthcoming but 1994 saw the inevitable Greatest Hits package, *Our Town*, beat its stately path to the top of the album charts. Even then Sony couldn't resist another marketing ploy, adding a trio of unreleased songs to the set to make it all the more collectable, though to be fair this has become a pretty widespread move in record company circles.

Reviews were pretty favourable, Rob Beattie writing in *Q*, 'Deacon Blue's back catalogue [has] a seemingly inexhaustible supply of high-class singles . . . truly earcatching adult pop.' Craig McLean meanwhile told *Vox* readers, 'Terminal leanings to the over-earnest have made Ricky Ross an almost pathologically loathed figure in some circles, but there is no doubt that the man can write songs . . . the closing "In The Mood" a clear example of what Deacon Blue do best: quiet, ruminative and humble AOR.'

With the album installed at No. 1, the accompanying concert tour turned into a Greatest Hits package, Ross finally returning to the songs like 'Real Gone Kid' and 'Fergus Sings the Blues' which had inadvertently wreaked such havoc with his musical career. Was the album a punctuation mark, signalling the end of the first phase of Deacon Blue's development or was it something more final? The news leaked out at the end of April when it was announced that Dougie Vipond had accepted a job as a presenter on Scottish Television's arts-entertainment show *N.B.* Ross had already gone on record as saying, 'I'm only one-sixth of a working unit. I couldn't see the day that Deacon Blue could continue if one of us were to leave. It's either the six of us or nothing at all.'

Vipond having already sorted out a new career for himself, it's clear that the decision to quit had been taken some time earlier, probably around the time the November 1993 tour was called off. With their position as one of Britain's biggest groups still intact, a point reinforced by the enormous success of *Our Town* which was another platinum seller with sales in excess of 300,000, it seemed inconceivable that the group should split up. However, it's apparent that various forces had conspired to eat into their resolve to the point at which, for the sake of their friendship, time had to be called.

On a personal level, they'd been together eight years without changing the line-up and had endured an intensive working schedule through that time. Personality conflicts were inevitable even if short-lived. Ricky and Lorraine had the added pressure of parenthood to deal with and it's likely that their commitment to that lifestyle rather than the rock 'n' roll one led to a lessening in their interest in touring and maintaining the band. In turn, a failure to tour and tour and then tour some more meant that the likelihood of their eventually breaking through in America was very much reduced, even if Ross still retained it as an ambition. 'Despite what we've achieved,' he said prior to the release of *Our Town*, 'I'm still very ambitious where Deacon Blue is concerned. And that involves America. No Scottish band has been really successful there, not even Simple Minds.' The dawning realization that America would not fall under their spell must have placed the final nail in the group's coffin.

The farewell tour turned into a passionate occasion, of course, though John Williamson wrote perceptively in the *Glasgow Herald* that, 'For a band that thrived on its on-stage energy, this is a heads down straight run-through of the many hits which works as a result of its execution more than its content. In doing so it also highlights the reasons for their success and also their demise . . . in the audience there are tears and loudmouth record company people expel gallons of high volume hot air during the quiet songs.' Ross had been philosophical before that final Glasgow show saying, 'The last night of any tour is always that bit special, but this one will be even more so. Live at the Barrowland in Glasgow. In front of our true fans. I'm trying not to make too big a deal out of it, but of course it will be emotional. A few tears? Probably.'

Some might scoff that Ross was derivative to the end, quoting the Quiet One in his resignation note, but it summed things up nicely: 'As George Harrison once said, all things must pass,' Ross announced after three million album sales. 'We're leaving on a high with no plans to work together after the tour.'

CHAPTER FOURTEEN

How did things fall apart within Deacon Blue after what has to be regarded as a pretty short career – eight years and just four studio records? It's easy to point a finger at those who could be to blame, but the principals must all take a share; the press, Deacon Blue itself and the record company.

The music press are often looked at as some diabolic force that came into being purely to destroy the careers of promising groups – anyone who's ever read anything by Julie Burchill will take the point. Realistically though, the press, especially the weekly variety, are motivated to go to extremes simply because of their need to generate sufficient worthwhile news to fill the pages. When a group is starting and has been latched on to by a newspaper, then that artist is fawned over during a brief honeymoon period. For that short while, said group is the greatest band ever to have plugged in a guitar, they're the future of rock music and their advent may even herald the Second Coming.

Once a band has been around a while, especially if it's sold a lot of records, its members are dismissed as tedious old farts, irredeemable bastions of a bogus establishment that is ruining the country and stunting our children's growth. If you compound this infamy by actually making a lousy record too, then the world caves in on you. Once a band gets to that stage, there is very little chance of turning the clock back unless you happen to be U2 or Neil Young. Deacon Blue were given no hope of a way back, in spite of employing Oakenfold and Osborne, as hip a couple of producers as you could possibly find circa 1993. For Deacon Blue the deed had already been done, the poisoned chalice taken, the Faustian pact signed or whatever other cliché you choose to employ. Let's face it, in terms of credibility, Deacon Blue were ranked one notch below the Singing Nun.

In truth, journalists were fulfilling the function for which they were employed and anyone happy to read the acres of newsprint given over to good reviews in the early days had better be big enough to cope with the brickbats that will finally start to fly. As Ross accepted, 'Everyone is happy to encourage a nice, wee band who are the equivalent of Blackburn Rovers trying to get up from the second division. But who likes Blackburn Rovers now?'

The greatest thing about joining the establishment, of finding your name on the Virgin 1215 playlist alongside Dire Straits, Simply Red and Whitney Houston is that, if that's the music you're aspiring to, you don't actually need the press because you've got your audience already. If you want to pack arenas and wallpaper the bathroom with platinum records, the establishment is the place to be – ask Cliff or Eric or Elton. You might never be considered trendy but if that's your kind of music and you're getting well rewarded for it, why worry?

For Ricky Ross and Deacon Blue, the difficulty arose when they found out, a little late in the day, that the establishment wasn't all it was cracked up to be and that the admission fee was far higher than they were prepared to pay. The need to become larger than life, to become a rock star, to constantly play the game was something they were not aware of in advance and once the dawning realization came, it was too late to bail out. Or rather, they bailed out but the press was happy to see them drown, distrusting the band's artistic motives for wanting to stay afloat.

At the back of all this sits the record company with their sales charts, income projections and box of gimmicks. All they are saying is give us a hit. And once they had a few hits to work with, they were galvanized into action, trampling all over the reputation for fairness and honesty that their charges had built up with their fans.

Ricky Ross has to bear a deal of the responsibility for the invidious position in which Deacon Blue eventually found themselves. As we've already seen, he was an ambitious man right from the start of Deacon Blue's ascent to success; his music was initially aspirational, hewn out of hope to lift the spirits of a blue-collar constituency that Ross, if not a part of, sympathized with. As a youngster in Dundee, growing up within the Brethren religion, he had seen the effects of poverty, and had helped out with disadvantaged children. He had then gone on to teach in Glasgow where he came further into contact with those less well-off than himself.

Like many of his background, he wanted to improve the lot of those lower down the social order but was equally keen that he should not end up in the same financially impecunious position himself. Thus his twin motivations as a songwriter were to chart the lives and loves of 'ordinary' people, attempting to ensure that these people were not forgotten, while creating a musical form that was sufficiently popular to bring him success. He later told *Vox*, 'I heard John Peel once say on the radio that he wished most rock groups could be born and then die very quickly, and I thought, "Only someone with a pensionable job at the BBC would say that." It takes into account absolutely nothing of the kind of things musicians have to go through. It illustrated for me that musicians and critics are looking for two completely different things.'

Ross did win a reputation as someone who was wary of the press and the two treated each other with a guarded aggression through the release of Deacon Blue's first album and the early singles from *When the World Knows Your Name*. By the time the band were ensconced in Wembley Arena and releasing EPs consisting of Bacharach & David songs, hostilities were out in the open. If Ross felt hard done by, he was also feeling increasingly unhappy with the stadium format as were the rest of the group.

Again, his upbringing and regard for people on a wider level suggested that his music should try to embrace everyone, and in so doing, he rationalized the concept of stadium rock and even looked forward to taking part in that particular circus. With those particular personal leanings, Ross was a godsend for CBS, someone with melodic songs that could be pushed into the anthemic field with the addition of a few major choruses here and there and the occasional tweak via a high profile remix. Encouraging all of Ross' pronouncements about stadium rock, pumping him with the plaudits that Springsteen and U2 had won for their work in those arenas, CBS were priming Ross for stadium stardom in the shortest possible time. Yet this ignored some salient facts – U2 didn't reach the arenas until their fourth studio record, *The Unforgettable Fire*. Springsteen had been playing for many, many years before he reached that point in his career too.

Deacon Blue in contrast were pushed to produce a hit album brimming with singles far too early and despatched to the arenas before they were ready, playing a record they no longer felt any empathy with; just as destructively, Ross in particular found himself ill at ease with the scale of the events, an inevitable outcome for one more intrigued by the smaller, introspective song. Stadium-sized rock needs a complete belief in the format and in what you are doing. Unfortunately, perhaps to his credit, Ross could never come to terms with the cultivation of the ludicrously inflated ego required, looking self-conscious and embarrassed by the events, clearly longing for the days of theatres and clubs.

If the executives back at CBS were busily inspecting the coffers, Ross and the band were inspecting their shredded integrity. Having not been able to say 'no' sufficiently loudly in 1988/9, they were quick to say that from here on in, they were going to do things their own way. The trouble was, by now, Deacon Blue were programmed for America, something which still held its allure for the band in romantic terms as the home of the music but also as a financial goal. The reaction to over-exposure, *Fellow Hoodlums* was a record that delighted the group and their longer-standing supporters but one which would have little chance of translating to American audiences as a consequence of its stout refusal to go inter-continental but rather reflect on their own lives and the city that surrounded them.

America was no longer a realistic option, especially when the fourth album, *Whatever You Say, Say Nothing* stuck to a decidedly British idiom of indie-dance, a form that has made little impact elsewhere. As a record it was fresh and exciting, a real departure for the group but by now they were boxed into a little pigeonhole that no one would allow them to escape from, while the record company, unhappy with the changes in the band's fortunes, were unwilling to promote them properly.

Right from the beginning CBS had seen Deacon Blue as the goose that might lay a batch of golden eggs and for a brief period, such was the case. But CBS failed to see that in this band they had six mature individuals who had a good idea of what they wanted out of life and how they wanted to get it, not a bunch of kids they could groom into the latest teen sensation. With their heavy promotion of *Raintown*, they launched the group's career to a chorus of disapproval from those who fought shy of such blatant mercenary behaviour tainting the forces of art. The record company were never to learn the lessons of this and served only to alienate the fans the band already had, and the press who could have been allies in a musical rebirth.

Eventually, you have to conclude that rather than dying of natural causes at a good old age, Deacon Blue were beaten to death by the demands of an unforgiving music industry, a prime case of killing that golden goose. A band that could and should have been nurtured carefully, growing in small and manageable steps, might have been entering Wembley Arena for the first time eight years on, able to cope with both its scale and the inherent stupidity of the occasion. But like everything in Thatcher's vision of the eighties, the guiding principle was get rich quick – if you get rich enough quickly enough, you don't have to worry about the long-term. With a group that were politically unsympathetic to that view and artistically not ready for the adulation, that principle squeezed the life from them and closed the door on the band's future.

Ross was so disenchanted with the way things had progressed, he was to say, 'I don't know what I will do. I haven't made any plans. I wouldn't be sad if I didn't make another record.' By 1993, Deacon Blue were artistically stifled, critically crippled and commercially collapsing. The final straw came with *Our Town* when the company insisted on releasing 'Dignity' for the *third* time as a single to promote this new record along with a host of other advertising gimmicks, a ploy which sickened Ross.

'The last album [*Whatever You Say, Say Nothing*] was like someone getting in a car and driving it off a bridge. Sink or swim. Commercially we sank – it didn't do well at all. But I know one of its tracks, "Bethlehem's Gate" is the best song I've ever written and "Your Town" is the best single we've ever done. I think it should have been our biggest selling LP but it was the least successful. That made it strange when we came to our Greatest Hits package, because the most came from the record I liked least [*When the World Knows Your Name*]. If it sells a lot, I know I'm going to get the pressure of, "So now you know what people are looking for from the band." But I'm determined not to take any lessons from it . . . you have an album that sells a million and an album that only goes gold and it seems like a commercial hiccup. But in fact, it's still an awful lot of people still coming to see you.'

Since Deacon Blue were such a blatantly commercial concern in the eyes of the record company, the only way to win that freedom was to stop the band. The musicians will all surely surface again at some point, either in new bands or as session players or producers, for they are far too accomplished to disappear into obscurity. The bigger question is what will happen to Ross, the chief songwriter in the band? Having wriggled free of the burden that Deacon Blue became, he is unlikely to play the commercial game again with quite so much vigour – the likelihood of him working with Sony again is quite small, it seems. As a compulsive songwriter, he now has sufficient clout within the industry to work in that capacity, providing material for other singers, though whether this alone would be enough for him is open to doubt. In the fullness of time, there is every chance that he will reappear in the role of solo artist, albeit on a smaller scale, playing theatre concerts to an audience that is as fiercely attuned to his muse as in the earliest days of Deacon Blue.

What then did Deacon Blue achieve? Certainly they were one of the most successful bands of their time with three million sales attesting to that. The impression remains that they could have achieved far more, certainly in an artistic sense. Although it was by far their most popular record, *When the World Knows Your Name* might, in retrospect, be regarded as a commercial disaster and an artistic waste, condemning the group to a position in the public mind as purveyors of slick, deep and meaningless pop, a reputation they did not deserve.

There were many who loathed everything that Deacon Blue did. David Belcher, a columnist in their native Glasgow, had little time for the band. Penning an obituary to the group, he argued, 'There was always something dubious about their wider claims to an artistic identity. Ricky is ever the sensible Dundonian trying to be a gallus Glaswegian trying to be a streetwise New Yorker. A secondary-school teacher bidding to be a blue-collar pug. Him and his Deacs acted big and tough, but they wurny . . . I must say that Deacon Blue committed their worst sin in 1991 when Ricky publicly disavowed his own pop hit past, scorned the SECC's masses and told his audience he'd grown out of what they liked. Big sales figures weren't sufficient: Deacon Blue wanted critical respect and to be anointed with the unction of hipdom too.' Drawing an historic parallel with Deacon Brodie, an eighteenth-century citizen of Edinburgh,

Belcher wrote, 'Deacon Brodie infamously employed civic respectability to mask a life of theft and deception. He was hung in 1788 on a new form of gallows which he'd devised. And I don't need to tell you how to draw an analogy from that for Deacon Blue's expiry.'

Certainly it was fair enough to attack the band and Ross in particular for their wholesale appropriation of influences, most notably the use of Springsteen- and U2-style imagery on stage. Yet Ross refused to countenance that as a failure, ascribing more pragmatic considerations to it. 'Anybody who knows anything about pop music knows that the great books have all been written by Chuck Berry, John Lennon or Lieber and Stoller. I knew we'd never be flavour of the decade because we weren't trying to do something really new. We were trying to be all the things we'd loved, which is why I wore a vest and played for three hours on stage, to see if we could beat Bruce Springsteen. I saw a promotional poster once which said "Nothing in the world sounds like Prefab Sprout" but I've never wanted us to sound like nothing. The reason I like the Beatles is because they remind me of Chuck Berry. I want everything in the world to sound like Deacon Blue. And I want us to be full of all the things I like.'

You could rightly accuse Ross of a lack of ambition – if you're unlikely to find the lost chord, you might at least try. It seemed that his aspirations were on a social level, a hope that things would improve for his fellow citizens. It was a pity that he did not aspire to creating something highly original for as a talented writer, it was a challenge to which he could have risen over time. When Ross went in search of critical approbation at the tail end of the group's career, he really should have known that his earlier proclamations, his unashamed desire to usurp his heroes, to become a younger Van Morrison, has disqualified him from similar heroic status; rock's legends have all carved out a unique little niche for themselves on the fringes of rock's boundaries. It appears that this was a fact of life to which he and the band found it hard to reconcile themselves.

Ross spoke affectionately of the band as a whole, describing it by saying, 'I think we're plodders in the sense that as individuals, as people, as a band we get here . . . there are one or two people in the band where there's absolutely no doubt about their talent and the fact that they could do things on their own. But what Deacon Blue are good at and what I'm good at is working together and creating something that's bigger than the sum of its parts.' Critics might well agree. Deacon Blue were craftsmen, artisans rather than artists. They knew their way round a serviceable hook, had an ear for a great chorus, knew a thing or two about melody and were sufficiently tasteful to borrow from the right places, but never really threatened to turn the music into their own, never seemed likely to put their indelible stamp on the culture of rock music. Other groups have stolen far more obviously and ruthlessly from the past but by means of denial or a little camouflage have got away with it. Ricky Ross never made any bones about the fact that he wanted to be a second-generation Springsteen – such honesty is rarely forgiven in an industry built on artifice.

For such a large band, internal conflict had been kept at a fairly low level, possibly because Ross had been identified as the leader early on. Ewen Vernal accepted the position, saying, 'It's good to have someone like that, someone who has a clear direction about what he wants to do musically. And Ricky's got so much energy, buzzing around, he's not afraid of trying different things.'

The impressive group chemistry was a potent force in keeping the band together, but it was also a factor in the final break-up of the group. Ross admitted, 'After eight good years, it seemed the natural thing to do. Why not go out on a high? We're selling records, the tour is sold out. It felt like time to go. Most bands split, then leave months of hurt behind them. Not us. It's nice to know that we're all still speaking to each other. And we are. No one is arguing.'

Keen not to ruin that friendship simply to go through the motions of recording once more, Ross added, 'We've made four albums we're all really proud of. For eight years we've done exactly what we wanted to do. It's been a nice relationship. All six of us have been together all of the time. Beyond Deacon Blue we'll still be friends. We'll stay in touch. But was there another Deacon Blue album in us? That was the real question. I don't think so. It's maybe time we all found our feet individually. Meet other people and do something new. We need a change.'

Friendship was, as you would expect, an important consideration for Ross, a man who stuck to his principles. 'I'm constantly amazed at the strength of friendships,' he told *Hot Press* in 1989. 'People who are really good friends now have been for a long, long time and I'm glad that I've managed to keep that. It's been as much an effort on their part as it has been on mine. For a while, when you first start doing things and you'd go to people's houses and there was a tendency for them to go, "Oh, that's all right for you, you're off doing this and that," but you've got to get beyond that level. You can't be bothered apologizing for what you do all the time, so with really good friends they know that if we're off doing a TV show that you're up first thing in the morning, hanging around all day . . . they realize it's just a job.' By 1994, that job was becoming too much of a chore for Ricky Ross and Deacon Blue.

The group had been formed for fun and also as a way out of dead-end jobs and Glaswegian dole queues. With *When the World Knows Your Name* such a big seller, there were few immediate financial insecurities. With that worry gone, once the trials and tribulations of being in a band drained the fun out of it, there was no sensible reason to continue.

Back in February 1986 just as Deacon Blue were in the early stages of formation, one of Ricky Ross' songwriting heroes, Elvis Costello, reached the singles charts with 'Don't Let Me Be Misunderstood'. It's a cry that Ross might have let slip over the last decade – some see that as pretentiousness, others an attempt to inject some sincerity and honesty into rock 'n' roll. Whatever the case, the last words must belong to Ross. 'Look, I don't want people to buy my records because they've had good reviews. I want them to buy them because they've heard them on the radio. And I don't want to be one of those acts the critics love who are famous for being ironic and taking the piss 'cos what are you gonna do for the rest of yer life, pal? Did you pick up the guitar to be clever or so that people will fall in love?'

DISCOGRAPHY

SINGLES

DIGNITY / Riches / Ribbons And Bows / Excerpts from *Raintown*
March 1987

LOADED / Long Distance From Just Across the Road / Which Side Are You On / Kings of the Western World
June 1987

WHEN WILL YOU (MAKE MY TELEPHONE RING) / Church / Town to be Blamed / Angeliou
August 1987

DIGNITY / Suffering / Just Like Boys / Ronnie Spector / Raintown (Piano Version) / Shifting Sand
January 1988 Chart: 31

WHEN WILL YOU (MAKE MY TELEPHONE RING) / That Brilliant Feeling No. 1 / That Brilliant Feeling No. 2 / That Brilliant Feeling No. 3 / Disneyworld / Punch and Judy Man
March 1988 Chart: 34

CHOCOLATE GIRL / S.H.A.R.O.N. / Dignity / Love's Great Fears / The Very Thing
July 1988 Chart: 43

REAL GONE KID / Little Lincoln / Real Gone Kid (Extended) / Born Again / It's Not Funny Anymore
October 1988 Chart: 8.

WAGES DAY / Take Me to the Place / Wages Day (Long Version) / Take the Saints Away / Trampolene
February 1989 Chart: 18

FERGUS SINGS THE BLUES / Long Window to Love / Fergus Sings the Blues (Long Version) / London A to Z / Back Here in Beano Land.
May 1989 Chart: 14

LOVE AND REGRET / Down in the Flood / Down in the Flood (Minimal Mix) / Undeveloped Heart / Love and Regret (Live) / Spanish Moon (Live) / Down in the Flood (Live) / Dark End of the Street (Live) / When Will You (Make My Telephone Ring) (Live)
September 1989 Chart: 28

QUEEN OF THE NEW YEAR / My America / Circus Lights (Acoustic) / Sad Loved Girl / Las Vegas / Chocolate Girl (Live) / Queen of the New Year (Live) / Undeveloped Heart (Live) / A Town to be Blamed (Live)
December 1989 Chart: 21

FOUR BACHARACH & DAVID SONGS EP: I'll Never Fall In Love Again / The Look of Love / Are You There (With Another Girl) / Message to Michael
August 1990 Chart: 2

YOUR SWAYING ARMS / Fourteen Years / Your Swaying Arms (Extended Mix) / Faifley
May 1991 Chart 23

TWIST AND SHOUT / Good / I'm Down / Golden Bells
July 1991 Chart: 10

CLOSING TIME / Friends of Billy Bear / I Was Like That / Into the Night
October 1991 Chart: 42

COVER FROM THE SKY / What Do You Want the Girl To Do / Christmas (Baby Please Come Home) / Loaded / One Hundred Things / Real Gone Kid
December 1991 Chart: 31

YOUR TOWN / Almost Beautiful / I've Been Making Such a Fool / Your Town (Extended Mix)
November 1992 Chart: 14

WILL WE BE LOVERS / Sleeper / Paint It Red / Will We Be Lovers (Norty 12") / Will We Be Lovers (DB Mix) / Will We Be Lovers (People's Mix) / Will We Be Lovers (Sally's Dub) / Will We Be Lovers (Spag Tek)
February 1993
Chart: 21

ONLY TENDER LOVE / Pimp Talking / Cracks You Up / Your Town (Perfecto Mix) / Riches / Which Side Are You On / Shifting Sand
April 1993 Chart: 34

I WAS RIGHT AND YOU WERE WRONG / Mexico Rain / Going Back (Live) / Wages Day / I Was Right and You Were Wrong (Extended Mix) / Kings of the Western World / Suffering / Raintown (Piano Version).
April 1994. Chart: 20

ALBUMS

RAINTOWN
Born in a Storm / Raintown / Ragman / He Looks Like Spencer Tracy Now / Loaded / When Will You (Make My Telephone Ring) /

Chocolate Girl / Dignity / The Very Thing / Love's Great Fears / A Town to be Blamed
May 1987
Rereleased with free LP

RICHES

Which Side Are You On / Kings of the Western World / Angeliou / Just Like Boys / Raintown (Piano Version) / Riches / Church / Shifting Sand / Suffering / Ribbons and Bows / Dignity
August 1988 Chart: 14

WHEN THE WORLD KNOWS YOUR NAME

Queen of the New Year / Wages Day / Real Gone Kid / Love and Regret / Circus Lights / This Changing Light / Sad Loved Girl / Fergus Sings the Blues / The World Is Lit By Lightning / Silhouette / One Hundred Things / Your Constant Heart / Orphans
April 1989 Chart: 1

OOH LAS VEGAS

Disneyworld / Ronnie Spector / My America / S.H.A.R.O.N. / Undeveloped Heart / Souvenirs / Born Again / Down in the Flood / Back Here in Beano Land / Love You Say / Let Your Hearts Be Troubled / Gentle Teardrops / Little Lincoln / That Country (Beneath Your Skin) / Is It Cold Beneath the Hill? / Circus Lights / Trampolene / Las Vegas / Killing the Blues / Long Window To Love / Christine / Take Me To the Place (For Oscar Marzaroli) / Don't Let the Teardrops Start
September 1990 Chart: 3

FELLOW HOODLUMS

James Joyce Soles / Fellow Hoodlums / Your Swaying Arms / Cover From the Sky / The Day That Jackie Jumped the Jail / The Wildness / A Brighter Star Than You Will Shine / Twist and Shout / Closing Time / Goodnight Jamsie / I Will See You Tomorrow / One Day I'll Go Walking
June 1991 Chart: 2

DEACON BLUE

WHATEVER YOU SAY, SAY NOTHING

Your Town / Only Tender Love / Peace & Jobs & Freedom / Hang Your Head / Bethlehem's Gate / Last Night I Dreamed of Henry Thomas / Will We Be Lovers / Fall So Freely Down / Cut Lip / All Over the World
March 1993 Chart: 4

OUR TOWN – THE GREATEST HITS

Dignity / Wages Day / Real Gone Kid / Your Swaying Arms / Fergus Sings the Blues / I Was Right and You Were Wrong / Chocolate Girl / I'll Never Fall In Love Again / When Will You (Make My Telephone Ring) / Twist and Shout / Your Town / Queen of the New Year / Only Tender Love / Cover From the Sky / Love and Regret / Beautiful Stranger / Will We Be Lovers / Loaded / Bound to Love / Still in the Mood
1994 Chart: 1

SOURCES

THE GLASGOW EVENING TIMES:

Singing the Blues by Fraser Middleton, 19 May 1994.

THE GLASGOW HERALD:

Singing Double Act Awakes to Dreaming by David Belcher, 21 March 1991.

Salvoes From Out of the Blue by David Belcher, 28 May 1991.

Live review, Glasgow Royal Concert Hall by Peter Easton, 2 January 1992.

Live review, Glasgow Barrowland by David Belcher, 3 April 1993.

Downfall of the Deacons by David Belcher, 13 May 1994.

Singing the Blues by Billy Sloan, 13 May 1994.

Live review, Glasgow Barrowland by John Williamson, 21 May 1994.

THE GUARDIAN:

Live review, Edinburgh by Bob Flynn, 4 April 1988.

Live review, Wembley Arena by Caroline Sullivan, 13 September 1990.

Fellow Hoodlums LP review by Adam Sweeting, 6 June 1991: © the *Guardian*.

HOT PRESS:

Tangled Up in Blue by George Byrne, 18 May 1989.

Bringing Home the Deacon by Paul Cleary, 27 June 1991.

DEACON BLUE

MELODY MAKER:

Live review, Glasgow Community Central Hall by Tom Morton, 20 April 1985.

Live review, Glasgow Club Eden by Tom Morton, 8 March 1986.

Blue For You by Tom Morton, 29 March 1986.

Live review, Glasgow Royal College of Music & Drama by Tom Morton, 21 June 1986.

Live review, London Marquee by Mat Smith, 29 November 1986.

Story of the Blues by Tom Morton, 13 December 1986.

Keeping Faith by Jonh Wilde, 4 April 1987.

Live review, Harlesden Mean Fiddler by Angie Daniell, 6 June 1987.

The Great Escape by Mat Smith, 4 July 1987.

Live review, Shetland Rock Festival by Tom Morton, September 1987.

Shrink Rap – Lorraine McIntosh, 31 October, 1987.

Live review, London Town & Country Club by Paul Oldfield, 19 December 1987.

Live review, Liverpool Royal Court by Penny Kiley, 9 April 1988.

Live review, London Dominion Theatre by Andrew Smith, 5 November 1988.

The Reluctant Tourist by Ian Gittins, 8 April 1989.

Live review, Wembley Arena by Ian Gittins, 6 January 1990.

Live review, Wembley Arena by Zane, 29 September 1990.

NEW MUSICAL EXPRESS:

Live review, Dundee Dance Factory by Bob Flynn, 13 December 1986.

Raiders of the Lost Art by Adrian Thrills, 25 April 1987.

Raintown LP review by Len Brown, 30 May 1987.

Ricky's Hung Up by Andrew Jackson, 7 May 1988.

Live review, CND Benefit, Meadowbank Stadium by Alastair McKay, 20 August 1988.

Live review, Dundee Caird Hall by Jonathan Romney, 12 November 1988.

When the World Knows Your Name LP review by Andrew Collins, 8 April 1989.

Hello Blue World by Andrew Collins, 22 April 1989.

Ooh Las Vegas LP review by Terry Staunton, 22 September 1990.

Q:

Raintown LP review by Adam Sweeting, June 1987.
When the World Knows Your Name LP review by Map Snow, April 1989.
The Pilgrim's Progress by Mat Snow, June 1989.
Ooh Las Vegas LP review by Johnny Black, November 1990.
The Big Picture video review by Mat Snow, January 1991.
Fellow Hoodlums LP review by Rob Beattie, July 1991.
Glasgow Skyline by Robert Sandall, August 1991.
Whatever You Say, Say Nothing LP review by John Aizlewood, March 1993.
Our Town LP review by Rob Beattie, May 1994.

RECORD MIRROR:

Live review, London Marquee by Lesley O'Toole, March 1987.
Real Gone Kids by Andy Strickland, October 1988.

SELECT:

Ooh Las Vegas LP review by Andrew Harrison, November 1990.
Fellow Hoodlums LP review by Nick Griffiths, July 1991.

SMASH HITS:

Bitz, 18 July 1987.

SOUNDS:

Blue For You by Robin Gibson, 28 March 1987.
Raintown LP review by Mat Snow, 23 May 1987.
Blue Angel by Roger Holland, 4 July 1987.
Live review, London Marquee by Damon Wise, 25 July 1987.
Live review, Wembley Arena by George Berger, 22 September 1990.

THE SUNDAY TIMES:

Art exhibition, Peter Howson by Marina Vaizey, 11 October 1987: © The *Sunday Times*.

THE TIMES:

Live review, Wembley Arena by Jasper Rees, 12 September 1990.
Live review, Clapham Grand by David Sinclair, 8 March 1993.

Live review, Hammersmith Odeon by Alan Jackson, 23 December 1991: © *Sunday Times.*

VOX:

Ooh Las Vegas LP review by James Anthony, November 1990.
Work Rest and Pray by Martin Townsend, May 1991.
Fellow Hoodlums LP review by Craig McLean, July 1991.
Whatever You Say, Say Nothing LP review by Alan Jackson, April 1993.
Our Town LP review by Craig McLean, May 1994.
What's Your Problem? by Alan Jackson, May 1994.

INDEX

Abbey Road (album by Beatles), 20, 55
Aberdeen Exhibition Centre, 135
Achtung Baby (album by U2), 6, 166
Agnew, Harold, 67–8
Alexander, Mike, 134
Alive & Kicking (album by Simple Minds), 166
'All Over the World' (song by Ricky Ross), 165
'Are You There (With Another Girl)' (song by Ricky Ross), 145
ATV Songs, 32, 34, 45
Aztec Camera (Glasgow group), 23

Bacharach, Burt, 28–9
Band Aid, 133
Barrowlands Ballroom (Glasgow), 39, 170
Beatles, 9, 102, 164, 178
  album *Abbey Road*, 20, 55
  singles
    'Penny Lane', 27
    'Strawberry Fields Forever', 27
Beattie, Rob (of *Q*), 156
Belcher, David, 134, 167, 177
'Bethlehem's Gate' (song by Ricky Ross), 164, 176
Big Dish, 35, 40
Big Man, The (McIlvanney), 134
'Big Music, The', 81
Big Picture, The (video), 142
'Big Shoes' (song by Ricky Ross), 25
Big Sur, 46
Big Time (film), 168
Boardwalk (Manchester), 157
Bono (of U2), 18, 36, 160
  parallels with Ricky Ross, 14, 17, 19, 37
'Born in a Storm' (song by Ricky Ross), 63, 64, 67
'Brighter Star Than You Will Shine, A' (song by Pat Metheney), 153
Brodie, Deacon, 177–8
Brown, Len, 71
Burchill, Julie, 171

Cambridge Ball, 80
Cava Studios (Glasgow), 145
CBS (Columbia Broadcasting System), and Deacon Blue
    changing relationship, 99–100
    confidence in group, 52, 54–5
    contract, 10
    control of music, 73–4, 75
    exploitation of fans, 85
    first recordings, 51
    interest in group, 47–8, 50
    lack of sales, 82
    live performances, 70, 75
    marketing, 4, 7, 30

promotion, 76–7, 84–5
Raintown success, 86
release of singles, 62
unusual marketing, 94
take-over by Sony, 136, *see also* Sony
'Chairman Mao's Vacation' (song by Ricky Ross), 25n
Charlton, Gordon (of CBS), 47, 52
'Checkout Girls' (song by Ricky Ross), 25n
'Chocolate Girl' (single by Deacon Blue), 64–5, 86, 123, 138, 182
Christian Brethren Church
belief in financial security, 13–14
different from Plymouth Brethren, 11, 12
as evangelists/social workers, 12, 15
influence on Ricky Ross, 11, 12–13, 15, 18, 20
values and beliefs, 11, 12
Chrysalis record company, 30
'Circus Lights' (song by Ricky Ross), 115
Clapham Grand (London), 168
Clark, Petula, 27, 143
Clearmountain, Bob, 81, 83, 84
and Deacon Blue, 101, 114, 124
'Closing Time' (single by Deacon Blue), 184
'Closing Time' (song by Ricky Ross), 153
Club Eden (Glasgow), 35
CND (Campaign for Nuclear Disarmament), Deacon Blue benefit for, 108
Cole, Lloyd, 48, 91
Collins, Andrew, 107, 118
Collins, Edwyn, 23, 24
Collins, Phil, 25, 123
Costello, Elvis, 36, 124, 180
'Country Fair' (song by Van Morrison), 47
'Cover From the Sky' (single by Deacon Blue), 151, 184
'Cover From the Sky' (song by Ricky Ross), 151
Currie, Ken, 149
'Cut Lip' (song by Ricky Ross), 163, 165

Dance Factory (Dundee), 48
Daniell, Angie, 75–6
'Day that Jackie Jumped the Jail, The' (song by Ricky Ross), 152
de Burgh, Chris, 157
Deacon Blue
albums
Fellow Hoodlums, see Fellow Hoodlums (album by Deacon Blue)
Ooh las Vegas, 135, 185
Our Town – The Greatest Hits, see Our Town – The Greatest Hits (album by Deacon Blue)
Raintown, see Raintown (album by Deacon Blue)
Riches, 85, 185
Whatever You Say, Say Nothing, 5, 6, 162, 163, 165–6, 166–7, 186
When the World Knows Your Name, see When the World Knows Your Name (album by Deacon Blue)
and America, 124, 170
audiences, 3, 34–5, 39
and Bob Clearmountain, 101, 114, 124
can be trusted, 33–4
CBS (Columbia Broadcasting System) *see* CBS (Columbia Broadcasting System) and Deacon Blue
and CND, 108
commercial success, 1, 7–8
concerts
Dundee, 48
Glasgow, 170
Royal Concert Hall, 158
SECC, 126
tour postponed, 168
Wembley, 126
critical failure, 1, 7–8
expenses of start up, 47
and the fans, 128

in Glasgow, 43
group
  attacked at Reading festival, 109
  bass guitarist (Ewen Vernal), 44
  disbanded, 170, 179
  drummer (Dougie Vipond), 35, 87–8, 142, 153, 160, 164
  formed by Ricky Ross, 34–5
  friendship of, 180
  guitarist (Graeme Kelling), 43, 50, 64, 66, 115, 120–21, 162, 164
  as individualists, 8
  keyboard (James Prime), 40, 64, 115
  recruited from other bands, 46
  vocalist (Lorraine McIntosh), 3, 45, 48, 64, 76, 78, 151–2
humanity of, 2
image change, 92–3
ingredients for success of, 9
legacy, 8
marketing of, 4, 6, 7, 30
name, 34
and poll tax protests, 129
reviews by
  Melody Maker, 35, 41, 48, 49–50, 76, 78, 95, 138, 139
  New Musical Express, 48, 71, 91, 110
sales of 3 million albums, 177
singles
  'Chocolate Girl', 64–5, 86, 123, 138, 182
  'Cover From the Sky', 151, 184
  'Dignity', *see* 'Dignity' (single by Deacon Blue)
  'Extended Play', 139
  'Four Bacharach & David Songs EP', 5, 145, 173, 183
  'Loaded', 61, 62, 182
  'Real Gone Kid', *see* 'Real Gone Kid' (single by Deacon Blue)
  'Twist and Shout', *see* 'Twist and Shout' (single by Deacon Blue)
  'Wages Day', *see* 'Wages Day' (single by Deacon Blue)
  'When Will You (Make My Telephone Ring)', 65, 66, 86, 91, 182
  'Your Swaying Arms', 153, 162, 183
  'Your Town', 161–2, 176, 184
'Deportees' (song by Woody Guthrie), 26
Dexy's Midnight Runners, 50
'Dignity' (single by Deacon Blue), 38, 48, 56, 74, 182
  in charts, 83
  comments by *Melody Maker*, 56, 58
  commercial failure, 70, 71
  and politics of employment, 56–9, 62
  re-recorded, 82
  released for third time, 176
Docherty, Raymond (of Big Dish), 35
Dominion Theatre (London), 110
'Don't Let Me Be Misunderstood' (single by Elvis Costello), 180
'Don't Let the Teardrops Start' (song by Ricky Ross), 132, 137
'Don't Look Back' (song by Ricky Ross), 25n
'Don't You Forget About Me' (single by Simple Minds), 24
Dr Love, 34
Dreaming (songs for TV play) (Ross and McIlvanney), 134, 135, 137
Dylan, Bob, 29, 50, 72, 165

Easton, Peter, 158
'Echoes of Another World' (song by Ricky Ross), 25
Exclusive Brethren, 20
'Extended Play' (single by Deacon Blue), 139

Face Value (album by Phil Collins), 123
'Fall So Freely Down' (song by Ricky Ross), 162, 164
Fellow Hoodlums (album by Deacon Blue), 142, 145, 147, 152, 154–5, 185
  low key marketing, 153

recorded in Paris and Glasgow, 145, 146
review by
Guardian, 155
Q, 156
'Fellow Hoodlums' (song by Ricky Ross), 151
'Fergus Sings the Blues' (single by Deacon Blue), 126, 183
'Fergus Sings the Blues' (song by Ricky Ross), 116, 158, 169
Ferry, Brian, 83
Fleetwood Mac, 162
'Fly, The' (single by U2), 6
Flynn, Bob, 48, 95
'Four Bacharach & David Songs EP' (single by Deacon Blue), 5, 145, 173, 183
Frame, Roddy, 23, 24
Friends Again (Glasgow group), 29

'Gentle Teardrops' (song by Ricky Ross), 137
'Germans Are Out Today, The' (song by Ricky Ross), 25n
Gibson, Robin, 75
Gillespie, Bobby (of Primal Scream), 161, 163
Gittins, Ian, 126
Give Out But Don't Give Up (album by Primal Scream), 163
Glasgow Evening Times, 187
Glasgow Herald, 134, 167, 177
quoting Ricky Ross, 133, 147
review of
final Glasgow show, 170
Royal Concert Hall show, 158
Whatever You Say, Say Nothing, 167
'Goodnight Jamsie' (song by Ricky Ross), 154
Grant, James (of Love and Money), as guitarist of Friends Again, 29
Guardian, 113
review of
Deacon Blue, 95
Fellow Hoodlums, 155
Guggi (of Virgin Prunes), 17
Guthrie, Woody, 26

'Hang Your Head' (song by Ricky Ross), 164
Happy Mondays, 153, 161, 164
Harrison, George, 170
Hatful of Hollow, 137
'He Looks Like Spencer Tracy Now' (song by Ricky Ross), 67, 68, 108
Hendrix, Jimi, 28, 160
Hipsway, 24, 29, 43
Hot Press (magazine), 126, 150
quoting Ricky Ross, 91, 125, 180
Howson, Peter, 149
Humperdinck, Engelbert, 27
Hüsker Dü song 'It's Not Funny Anymore', 50, 111–12

'I Love You Like a Son' (song by Ricky Ross), 25, 25n
'I Was Right and You Were Wrong' (single by Deacon Blue), 184
'I Will See You Tomorrow' (song by Ricky Ross), 154
'I'll Never Fall in Love Again' (song by Ricky Ross), 145
'In the Mood' (song by Ricky Ross), 169
'Independance Day' (single by Bruce Springsteen), 19
'indie-dance', 160, 161
INXS, 160, 164
'Is It Cold Beneath the Hill?' (song by Ross/McIlvanney), 134
'It's Not Funny Anymore' (song by Hüsker Dü), 50, 111–12

Jackson, Alan, 40, 158, 166
'James Joyce Soles' (song by Ricky Ross), 150
Jesus (Glasgow group), 24, 40, 43
Johnson, Matt (of the The), 104
Jones, Tom, 27
Joyce, James, 150

Kahne, David, 116
Kelling, Graeme
and Christian Brethren, 44
comments on
Fellow Hoodlums, 142
When the World Knows Your Name (album by Deacon Blue), 121–2
as guitar for Deacon Blue, 43, 46, 50, 64, 66, 115, 120–21, 162, 164
Kelly, Jon (of CBS), 54, 91, 135, 145
Kelvingrove Art Gallery and Museum, 150
Kiley, Penny, 95
'Killing the Blues' (song by Ross/McIlvanney), 134

'Last Night I Dreamed of Harry Thomas' (song by Ricky Ross), 164
Lennon, John, 29, 102, 178
'Let Your Hearts Be Troubled' (song by Ross/McIlvanney), 134
Lieber and Stoller, 178
Like a Prayer (album by Madonna), 117
'Like a Rolling Stone' (Dylan), 50
'Little India' (song by Ricky Ross), 25n
Livesay, Warne (CBS), 114
'Loaded' (single by Deacon Blue), 61, 62, 95, 182
Lone Justice, 98
'Long Window to Love' (song by Ricky Ross), 97
'Look of Love, The' (song by Ricky Ross), 145
Love and Money, 29, 35, 40
'Love and Regret' (single by Deacon Blue), 126, 183
'Love and Regret' (song by Ricky Ross), 115, 126
'Love You Say' (song by Ross/McIlvanney), 134
'Love's Great Fears' (song by Ricky Ross), 66

MacAloon, Paddy (of Prefab Spout), 27, 113
Madchester's Stone Roses, 153, 167
Mainstream (album by Lloyd Cole), 91
Malone, Bernadette, 166
marketing of Deacon Blue, 4, 6, 7, 30
Marquee (London), 48, 71, 76, 98
Martyn, John, 25, 26, 64
Mary Chain (Glasgow group), 24, 40, 43
Marzaroli, Oscar, 121, 148–9
McCartney, Paul, 29, 102
McGlynn, Brian,
as singer with Woza, 23, 25–6
McGowan, Shane (of the Pogues), 116
McIlvanney, William (playwright), and Deacon Blue, 134, 152
McIntosh, Lorraine
birth of first child, 159
as Deacon Blue vocalist, 3, 45, 48, 64, 151–2
death of father, 154
with Ewan Vernal, 45–6
keeness to join Deacon Blue, 45–6
marriage to Ricky Ross, 141
not fully used as vocalist, 71, 111, 138–9
quoted by
Melody Maker, 65
New Musical Express, 46
views on
failure, 88
image, 139
love, 124
money, 88
pornography, 65
McKay, Alastair, 108, 112
McKee, Maria (of Lone Justice), 98, 111
McLean, Craig, 155–6, 169
Mean Fiddler (Harlesden), 76
Melody Maker, 86, 96
comments on 'Dignity', 56, 58
comments on 'Loaded', 95
quoting
Lorraine McIntosh, 65
Ricky Ross, 29, 64, 67

review of Deacon Blue, 35, 48, 78, 138, 139
at Dundee, 110
at Wembley, 126
'Message to Michael' (song by Ricky Ross), 145
Metheney, Pat, 153
Michael, George, 4, 122
Moore, Carol (of Talking Drums), 35
Morton, Tom (of *Melody Maker*), 25, 35, 41, 76
Moyet, Alison, 98
Music Week, 54

NEC (National Exhibition Centre) (Birmingham), 135 157
Nelson Riddle Orchestra, 150
New Musical Express (NME), 23, 86, 104
quoting
Lorraine McIntosh, 46
Ricky Ross, 33, 43
review of
Deacon Blue, 48, 71, 91, 110
Ooh Las Vegas, 136
When the World Knows Your Name (album by Deacon Blue), 107, 118
New Order (Manchester group), 24
Newman, Randy, 150
Nicaragua benefit, 15
'Nothing Compares 2 U' (song by Sinead O'Connor), 144

Oakenfold, Paul (Perfecto), 6, 161, 164–5, 172
O'Connor, Sinead, 144
Odeon Hammersmith, 39, 125, 158
Oldfield, Paul, 78, 79
'One Day I'll Go Walking' (song by Ricky Ross), 153
'One Hundred Things' (song by Ricky Ross), 116
'Only Tender Love' (single by Deacon Blue), 184
'Only Tender Love' (song by Ricky Ross), 164
Ooh Las Vegas (album by Deacon Blue), 135, 185
critical reviews, 136
marketing by Sony, 137
Orange Juice (Glasgow group), 23
'Orphans' (song by Ricky Ross), 116, 130, 150
Osborne, Steve (Perfecto), 6, 161, 164–5, 172
O'Toole, Lesley, 71
Our Town – The Greatest Hits (album by Deacon Blue), 176, 186
No.1 in charts and awarded platinum disc, 168–9
reviews, 169

Painted Word, 35, 47
Palmer, John (of Love and Money), 35
'Peace and Jobs and Freedom' (song by Ricky Ross), 162, 164, 165
Pellow, Marti (of Wet Wet Wet), 4
'Penny Lane' (single by Beatles), 27
Perfecto production team, 161
and *Whatever You Say, Say Nothing*, 163
Phonogram, 10
Pink Floyd, 2
Plymouth Brethren
belief in Scriptures, 11–12
and Bono of U2, 17
and Christian Brethren, 11, 12
and Exclusive Brethren, 20
formation of, 11
Pogues, 116
Politti, Scritti, 51
Postcard, 23, 24, 29
Prefab Sprout, 27, 35, 106, 178
Presley, Elvis, 26, 27
Primal Scream, 160
album *Give Out But Don't Give Up*, 163
Prime, James
as co-writer for Deacon Blue songs, 116, 139, 154
as keyboard for Deacon Blue, 40, 64, 115

Q (magazine), 59, 136, 142
quoting Ricky Ross, 11, 145

review of
Fellow Hoodlums, 156
Our Town – The Greatest Hits, 169
Whatever You Say, Say Nothing, 166
'Queen of The New Year' (single by Deacon Blue), 126, 183
'Queen of the New Year' (song by Ricky Ross), 114, 126, 158

Race of Angels (Waters), 38
'Ragman' (song by Ricky Ross), 63, 64
Raintown (album by Deacon Blue), 25, 62, 63, 69, 70, 79, 184
compared with *When the World Knows Your Name* album by Deacon Blue, 114
critical reviews, 71, 72, 73
as début album, 41
focus on Glasgow, 55
introspective, 105
as longer term success, 106
no follow-up, 92
promotion by CBS, 76–7
romantic, 64
success in charts, 86
'Raintown' (song by Ricky Ross), 25, 48, 62, 63, 64, 67
Rattle and Hum (album by U2), 19
Rattling the Cage (later Big Sur), 46
Reading Festival, Deacon Blue attacked by fans, 109
'Real Gone Kid' (single by Deacon Blue), 6–7, 103, 158, 183
press criticism, 108
success in charts, 108
supporting tour, 109–10
'Real Gone Kid' (song by Ricky Ross), 169
Lorraine McIntosh vocal, 111
record companies objectives, 102
Record Mirror, 66, 71, 109
critical review of Deacon Blue, 126
review of SECC show, 126
Reeves, Jasper, 138
religion
Christian Brethren Church
and Graeme Kelling, 44
and Ricky Ross, 11, 12–13, 15, 18, 20
see also Christian Brethren Church; Plymouth Brethren
Riches (album by Deacon Blue), 85, 185
rock music
belief in by Ricky Ross, 38, 51, 94
outdated?, 160–61
real meaning of, 2
spirituality of, 36
vicarious thrill from, 39
Rolling Stones, 38, 50, 83, 160, 163
Romney, Jonathan, 110
'Ronnie Spector' (song by Ricky Ross), 137
Ross, Ricky, *see also* Deacon Blue; McIntosh, Lorraine,
early years
born Dundee, 11
and Christian Brethren Church, 11, 12–13, 15, 18, 20
Dundee teacher training college, 14
enters music industry, 16–17, 18
faith as teenager, 13
first stage performance, 21
and folk music, 26
leaves teaching, 32
parents' attitude to pop, 12
and Protestant work ethic, 14, 41
school and security, 14
as Scottish patriot, 15–16
as teacher in Glasgow, 22, 23
with Woza
impressed by Friends Again, 29
on keyboard, 20, 23
leaves, 30
moves to Glasgow, 20
opinion of Springsteen, 19
parallels with Bono, 14, 17, 19, 37
as songwriter, 22–3, 25
with Deacon Blue
audience reactions, 37

collaboration with McIlvanney, 134–5
comparison of albums, 122
concern about strategy, 142–4
against dilettantism, 33
Dundee concert, 48
end of group, 170, 179
expense of starting, 47
formation, 34–5
illness, 78
as lead singer, 3, 10
and long term security, 42
marketing of albums with CBS, 4, 7, 30
personifies group, 4
and Phonogram, 10
quoted by
Hot Press, 91, 125, 180
Melody Maker, 29, 64, 67
New Musical Express, 33, 43
recruiting for group, 46
as songwriter, 3, 53, 100, 146–7
albums
So Long Ago, 25, 46
personal life
birth of first child, 159
divorce, 121, 123
marriage problems, 63
marriage to Lorraine McIntosh, 141
married to Zara *see* Ross, Zara, 2
views on
creating intimacy with audience, 112–13
elections, 80
fun night out, 87, 130
future career, 176–7
Glasgow as base, 125, 147–8
morality, 64
nuclear weapons, 68
politics of employment, 56–9
pop stars and politics, 133–4
problems of Glasgow, 43, 55, 60
record buying, 180–81
recorded music, 94
rock music, 38, 51, 53
Scottish nationalism, 130–32, 166
socialism, 61, 130
Ross, Zara (wife of Ricky Ross), 20
divorce, 121, 123
marriage problems, 63
Rowan, Derek *see* Guggi
Royal College of Music and Drama (Glasgow), 41
Royal Concert Hall (Glasgow), 158
Ryder, Shaun (of Happy Mondays), 161

'Sad Loved Girl' (song by Ricky Ross), 97, 116
'Sail Away' (song by Randy Newman), 150
Sandall, Robert, 14
Scott, Mike (of Waterboys), 29, 30, 48, 55
Scottish Assembly, 16
Scottish Presbyterian Church, 14
SECC, 126, 142, 157
Sedaka, Neil, 32
Select (magazine), 136, 155
'S.H.A.R.O.N.' (song by Ricky Ross), 137
'Silhouette' (song by Ricky Ross), 116, 123
Simple Minds, 83, 170
album *Alive & Kicking*, 166
'Big Music, The', 81
single 'Don't You Forget About Me', 24
Sinatra, Frank, 27, 32
Sinclair, David, 168
Sly Stone, 160
Smash Hits, 189
Smith, Andrew, 110
Smiths, 137
Smiths (Manchester group), 24
Snow, Mat (of Q), 11, 20, 48, 72, 142
review of *When the World Knows Your Name* (album by Deacon Blue), 119
So Long Ago (album by Ricky Ross), 25, 46
'Some People Last Winter' (song by Ricky Ross), 25, 25n
'Something About Ireland' (song by Ricky Ross), 25n

Sony
marketing of Deacon Blue, 4, 30, 136–7, 143
working with Ricky Ross, 177
see also CBS
Sounds (magazine), 72, 73, 75, 76, 84, 138
Springsteen, Bruce, 18
albums
Nebraska, 113
Tunnel of Love, 47
singles
'Independance Day', 19
'The Ties That Bind', 19
'stadium rock', 53, 112, 143
Staunton, Terry, 136
'Stranger at the Party' (song by Ricky Ross), 25
'Strawberry Fields Forever' (single by Beatles), 27
Style Council, 50
Sullivan, Caroline (of *Guardian*), 138
Sunday Times, 149
'Surprised By Joy' (song by Ricky Ross), 25n
Sweeting, Adam, 73, 155

Take Me Home (BBC production), 66
Talking Drums, 35
'Taste it' (song by INXS), 160
Taylor, James, 22
'That Country (Beneath Your Skin)' (song by Ricky Ross), 137
Thatcherism, 13, 15, 102, 115
The The, 104
'This Changing Light' (song by Ricky Ross), 115, 130
This is the Sea (album by Waterboys), 47
Thompson, Chris (of Friends Again), 29
Thompson, Richard, 151
Thrills, Adrian, 24, 51
'Ties That Bind, The' (single by Bruce Springsteen), 19
Times, The, 14, 138, 149, 158
review of show at Clapham Grand, 168
'Times They Are A-Changin'' (single by Bob Dylan), 165
Top of the Pops (TV programme), 108
Town and Country Club (London), 78, 79, 80
'Town to be Blamed, A' (song by Ricky Ross), 67, 79
'Trampolene' (song by Ricky Ross), 137
Tunnel of Love (album by Bruce Springsteen), 47, 123
'Twist and Shout' (single by Deacon Blue), 183
musical influences, 153
reaches top ten charts, 153

U2
albums
Achtung Baby, 6, 166
Joshua Tree, The, 103
Rattle and Hum, 19, 96
and book *Race of Angels*, 38
criticism by press, 96
singles
'Edge, The', 66, 167
'Fly, The', 6
'With or Without You', 103
U2 (group), 36, 133, 164
Usher Hall (Edinburgh), 129

Vaizey, Marina, 149
Van Morrison, 26, 124, 178
albums
Astral Weeks, 113
Veeden Fleece, 47
songs
'Angeliou', 50, 85
'Country Fair', 47
Veeden Fleece (album by Van Morrison), 47
Velvet Underground, 43
Vernal, Ewen
as bass guitar with Deacon Blue, 44
on bass with Woza, 23
as co-writer with Deacon Blue, 116, 179

'Very Thing, The' (song by Ricky Ross), 66
Vipond, Dougie
  Deacon Blue drummer, 35, 87–8, 142, 153, 160, 164
  leaves group, 169
'Vision On' (song by Ricky Ross), 25n
Vox (magazine), 40, 49, 136, 155, 173
  review of
    Our Town – The Greatest Hits, 169
    Whatever You Say, Say Nothing, 166

'Wages Day' single by Deacon Blue, 103, 112, 183
  chart success, 113
  satisfies Ricky Ross musically, 113–14
Waits, Tom, 168
Waterboys, 29
  album *This is the Sea*, 47
  and Ricky Ross, 30
Waters, John, 38
'Week in Politics, A' (song by Ricky Ross), 25n
Wembley Arena, 126, 135, 156, 157, 173
Wet Wet Wet, 4, 125
Whatever You Say, Say Nothing (album by Deacon Blue), 5, 6, 186
  at No.4 in the charts, 162
  and Perfecto, 163
  political/religious messages, 165–6
  reviews, 166–7
When the World Knows Your Name (album by Deacon Blue), 7, 18, 91, 92, 98, 185
  choice of title, 106–7
  comment by Lorraine McIntosh, 98
  commercial or musical motivation, 100–101
  compared with *Raintown*, 114
  group become unhappy with, 144
  new approach, 92–3, 97
  as No.1 in UK album charts, 117
  positive reviews, 118–19
  reactive, 105
  review by *New Musical Express*, 107
'When Will You (Make My Telephone Ring)' (single by Deacon Blue), 65, 66, 86, 91, 182
'Wildness The' (song by Ricky Ross), 151
'Will We be Lovers' (single by Deacon Blue), 184
'Will We be Lovers' (song by Ricky Ross), 163
Williamson, John, 170
Winwood, Muff (of CBS), 10, 48, 52, 85
'World is Lit by Lightning, The' (song by Ricky Ross), 123
Woza, 28
  bass guitar (Ewen Vernal), 23
  dissolved and reformed, 24
  end of the group, 29, 30
  formed in Glasgow, 20
  keyboard (Ricky Ross), 25
  singer (Brian McGlynn), 23
Woza Albert! (play), 23

'Your Constant Heart' (song by Ricky Ross), 116, 123
'Your Swaying Arms' (single by Deacon Blue), 153, 162, 183
'Your Swaying Arms' (song by Ricky Ross), 152
'Your Town' (single by Deacon Blue), 161–2, 176, 184